3

Put a picture of your dog
in this box

Your Dog's Name ....

Your Dog's License Number _____

 Date of Birth _____

Your Dog's Veterinarian _____

Address _____

Phone Number _____

Medications _____

Vet Emergency Number _____

Additional Emergency Numbers _____

 Feeding Instructions _____

Exercise Routine _____

 Favorite Treats _____

Tear me out!

YOUR ESSENTIAL *Poodle* INFORMATION SHEET

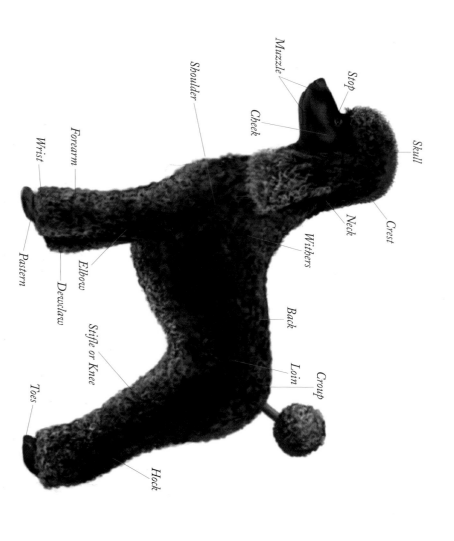

Muzzle

Stop

Shoulder

Cheek

Skull

Forearm

Wrist

Crest

Neck

Withers

Pastern

Elbow

Dewclaw

Back

Stifle or Knee

Loin

Croup

Toes

Hock

Meet the Poodle

■ Poodles come in three sizes: Toy, Miniature and Standard.

■ Poodles also come in an array of colors including white, black, brown, gray, blue, apricot, cream and more.

■ The Miniature and Standard Poodles are categorized by the American Kennel Club as Non-Sporting dogs, while the Toy Poodle is considered a member of the Toy group.

■ Despite their glamorous looks, Poodles were originally hard-working water dogs.

■ The word Poodle derived from the German word *pudel* or *pudelin*, which means "to splash in the water."

■ The Poodle's curly coat is actually water repellent, which helps keep him warm while dashing in and out of water.

■ Revered for his "almost human" intelligence and elegant, proud air, the Poodle is also down to earth and a great entertainer. His trainability and comic nature are what have made him a star performer in the circus and other entertainment venues.

■ Poodles require serious grooming due to a thick, harsh and curly top coat and a warm, wooly undercoat. Daily brushing and professional grooming are necessary.

■ Poodles love to be groomed. They sit calmly and enjoy the process.

■ Poodles are extremely devoted and are protective of their families.

Consulting Editor
IAN DUNBAR PH.D., MRCVS

Featuring Photographs by
WINTER CHURCHILL
PHOTOGRAPHY

Howell Book House

A Simon & Schuster Macmillan Company
1633 Broadway
New York, NY 10019

Macmillan Publishing books may be purchased for business or sales promotional use. For information please write: Special Markets Department, Macmillan Publishing USA, 1633 Broadway, New York, NY 10019.

Library of Congress Cataloging-in-Publication Data
       The essential Poodle / consulting editor, Ian Dunbar; featuring photographs by Kerrin Winter and Dale Churchill.
      p. cm.
  Includes index.
  ISBN 1-58245-020-X
  1. Poodles. I. Dunbar, Ian. II. Howell Book House
  SF429.P85E78 1999   98-42618
  636.72'8—dc21   CIP

Manufactured in the United States of America
10 9 8 7 6 5 4 3 2 1

Series Director: Michele Matrisciani
Book Design: Paul Costello
Photography: Courtesy of Diane Robinson: 74, 76–77
  All other photos by Winter Churchill Photography. Many poodles in interior photos courtesy of Donnchada Poodles.

ARE YOU READY?!

- ☐ Have you prepared your home and your family for your new pet?

- ☐ Have you gotten the proper supplies you'll need to care for your dog?

- ☐ Have you found a veterinarian that you (and your dog) are comfortable with?

- ☐ Have you thought about how you want your dog to behave?

- ☐ Have you arranged your schedule to accommodate your dog's needs for exercise and attention?

No matter what stage you're at with your dog—still thinking about getting one, or he's already part of the family—this Essential guide will provide you with the practical information you need to understand and care for your canine companion. Of course you're ready—you have this book!

THE ESSENTIAL

Poodle

The Poodle's Senses

SIGHT

Poodles can detect movement at a greater distance than we can, but they can't see as well up close. They can also see better in less light, but can't distinguish many colors.

SOUND

Poodles, like all dogs, can hear about four times better than we can, and they can hear high-pitched sounds especially well.

SMELL

A Poodle's nose is his greatest sensory organ. A dog's sense of smell is so great he can follow a trail that's weeks old, detect odors diluted to one-millionth the concentration we'd need to notice them, even sniff out a person under water!

TASTE

Poodles have fewer taste buds than we do, so they're more likely to try anything—and usually do, which is why it's important for their owners to monitor their food intake. Dogs are omnivorous, which means they eat meat as well as vegetables.

TOUCH

Poodles are social animals and love to be petted and played with. They especially love being groomed!

CHAPTER ONE

Getting to Know Your Poodle

Once you get to know the Poodle personality, it is not difficult to understand the dog's popularity throughout the ages. The Poodle is highly intelligent, active, good-natured and self-assured. It is a breed that carries itself with distinction, though many note that the Poodle has a sense of humor. The Poodle is suited to a show career, life in the field or life as household pet—adaptability few breeds can claim.

THE POODLE IS VERSATILE

Of these wonderful qualities, is there one that stands out? Again and again, breeders, enthusiasts, veterinarians—anyone who knows the

Poodle—remark on the dog's extraordinary intelligence.

For example, Poodles learn amazingly quickly. The ability to learn, and do so eagerly, is what enables the Poodle to fulfill the various roles—retriever, performer, show dog, excellent companion—he has had throughout his history.

Poodles excel at obedience training, whether learning basic house manners or working toward a Utility

CHARACTERISTICS OF THE POODLE

Highly intelligent

Good-natured

Suitable to a show career and life as a companion pet

Excellent at obedience training

Self-assured

Dignified

Active and energetic

title. As bright as the breed is, the Poodle has been the victim of misperception. Considered too "fancy" or "frilly," particularly by men, the amazing intellect of the Poodle has been often overlooked. And, perhaps understandably, some perception of the breed is linked to its unusual coat and trimmings. The hair styles are often perceived as frivolous. Don't be fooled by elaborate coat patterns, though. What is underneath all the fluff and puffs is anything but frivolous. Awaiting is a keen mind, ready and able to accomplish most any task.

Not only is the Poodle intelligent, he is also highly adaptable. He fits into the lifestyle and tempo of any household very well, whether the home be in the city or country, with or without children or other pets and the family small or large. In addition to his easy personality, the Poodle also comes in three sizes—Toy, Miniature and Standard. Owners can select a size that best fits their lifestyles and budgets.

The Poodle's flexibility even extends to how he relates to his owner. You will find little personality conflict with your Poodle because the Poodle modifies his personality to his owner. He is very sensitive to his owner, which is perhaps the result of his heritage as a hunting companion eagerly awaiting direction.

Underneath a fashionable coat is a very intelligent and able companion.

These Poodles express the fun-loving nature inherent to the breed.

The Poodle is often described as an active dog, though not hyperactive. He enjoys working as a retriever, being part of family activities, making a round in the show ring or just taking a walk through the neighborhood. And, in most cases, the Poodle works with tail-wagging exuberance.

Thick-headed and stubborn this breed is not. Rather, the Poodle is sensitive and, as mentioned previously, learns quickly. He has a unique ability to read situations and clues and respond appropriately. Once the dog knows and understands what is expected, he will comply happily. The Poodle is extremely eager to please his owner.

As noted in the Official Standard for the Poodle, the Poodle has an air of distinction and dignity peculiar to himself. Such characteristics are difficult to measure because they are subjective and open to interpretation; they could be considered anthropomorphic (attributing human characteristics to an animal) by some.

Those who understand and live with the breed are quick to describe the Poodle's personality as "dignified." The breed is known as neat, noble and stately. This is reflected in the way the Poodle carries himself and relates to people and his environment, most often with a head-up, tail-up attitude.

Contrasting with the Poodle's air of dignity is its playful, fun-loving streak. Described as a "sense of humor" by those who know and love the breed, the Poodle is well able to amuse owners with his antics. The ability to make people laugh, to perform, to suddenly break out of a "sophisticated" air, is probably why the breed excelled as a circus and stage performer.

COMPARING THE SIZES

A wonderful aspect of the Poodle is that he comes in three sizes, a sort of three-sizes-fits-all breed. Although the breed standard, excluding size, is the same for all three varieties, is it really the same dog?

For the most part, yes. Poodles of all sizes are intelligent, energetic and are comfortable in any type of loving environment. There are some differences to be aware of that can affect which variety one might choose. The differences are not really differences in the essence of the breed, but are rather by-products of the particular size. No size is a bad choice.

The Toy is considered highly portable, which contributes to its popularity. These dogs travel well, and, in spite of their small size, they are strong in spirit. The Toy has been described as a small version of the Standard; he obviously is not

capable of retrieving game and the like, however, even though he may think he can.

Unfortunately, perhaps because of their small, toylike appearance, many owners tend to spoil this variety. Size is no reason to disregard manners. Basic obedience training is essential for any Poodle.

Should families with children consider a Toy? Some believe that the larger Poodles are better able to handle the day-to-day roughhousing that may occur with children. Certainly, responsible children, supervised by an adult, can be trusted with the diminutive Toy.

The Miniature Poodle is also portable. He is a larger dog than the Toy, but he does not have the extra space requirements of the Standard. The Miniature is an ideal middle-of-the-road choice.

Enthusiasts say there is nothing like a Standard—and that is certainly true. But keep in mind that Standard Poodles are big dogs, requiring proper accommodations and exercise. This is not to say that a Standard cannot live happily in an apartment. As long as the owner is committed to daily walks and romps in the park, and does not intend

to leave the dog alone day and evening, he will be fine. It is not so much the environment but what the owner is willing to provide that is important.

Grooming is essential for any size Poodle, and the bigger the Poodle, the bigger, and more expensive, the grooming job. The differences among the varieties just in brushing time is considerable. Multiply that by bathing, drying, clipping and scissoring—it adds up quickly.

Poodles come in an array of colors, although black and white are the most common.

CHAPTER TWO

Homecoming

The temptation to buy or adopt a Poodle puppy impulsively can be overwhelming. Too often, though, owners bring home a puppy or dog without giving it much thought.

Dogs, as puppies and adults, have a variety of needs that owners are not always prepared to meet. Often a new owner does not really understand the basics of proper dog care.

To make both a Poodle puppy's arrival in a new home and life thereafter a happy one, owners must be prepared. Following are some basics to think about before bringing a puppy or adult Poodle home.

COMMITMENT AND RESPONSIBILITY

On average, dogs live about twelve years. That means that once the cute Poodle puppy crosses the threshold, the owner is, for the next twelve years or so, responsible for her daily care. This entails daily walks, feeding and brushing; weekly bed washing and trips to the pet supply store; monthly visits to the groomer; annual veterinary checkups; and so on. Vacations must be planned in advance with accommodations—a kennel stay or a house sitter—for the dog. Costly medical emergencies can arise, as well. The Poodle is also dependent upon her owner for companionship and training.

But do not be discouraged by all this. Be realistic. What a Poodle or any pet needs most is a committed, responsible owner. It is better to "just say no" to adopting a pet if commitment and responsibility are lacking, or if funds are limited. However, if you are willing to take on the challenge of daily caring for, and nurturing of, a Poodle, you will reap a bountiful harvest.

Change in Lifestyle: The First Year

With the adoption of a Poodle puppy or adult comes a change in lifestyle—your lifestyle. Dogs have special needs, at each stage of growth, and they are dependent upon their owners to fulfill them.

Puppies are especially demanding, with their short attention spans, curiosity, bursts of playfulness, teething troubles and lack of socialization and training.

The Poodle's most impressionable period is between 6 weeks and 6 months. During this time, a pup develops her social skills and attitudes toward life. Pups that are well socialized and exposed to a wide variety of situations grow up to be well-adjusted adults. Pups that play with other puppies develop a good attitude toward other dogs, which helps prevent aggressive tendencies and shyness in the adult dog. Pups that are handled lovingly by people will develop trust toward people in general.

Most puppies will chew. If this happens during teething periods, usually around 4 months, a chew toy is essential. Chewing behavior will cease as the puppy matures,

Both owner and Poodle are happiest when spending quality time together.

7

PUPPY ESSENTIALS

To prepare yourself and your family for your puppy's homecoming, and to be sure your pup has what she needs, you should obtain the following:

Food and Water Bowls: One for each. We recommend stainless steel or heavy crockery—something solid but easy to clean.

Bed and/or Crate Pad: Something soft, washable and big enough for your soon-to-be-adult dog.

Crate: Make housetraining easier and provide a safe, secure den for your dog with a crate—it only looks like a cage to you!

Toys: As much fun to buy as they are for your pup to play with. Don't overwhelm your puppy with too many toys, though, especially the first few days she's home. And be sure to include something hollow you can stuff with goodies, like a Kong.

I.D. Tag: Inscribed with your name and phone number.

Collar: An adjustable buckle collar is best. Remember, your pup's going to grow fast!

Leash: Style is nice, but durability and your comfort while holding it count, too. You can't go wrong with leather for most dogs.

Grooming Supplies: The proper brushes, special shampoo, toenail clippers, a toothbrush and doggy toothpaste.

but bad habits can develop. Teach youngsters to chew only acceptable items.

Puppies commonly urinate when they are excited or frightened. This is an involuntary act and should not be punished. When a youngster urinates in this manner, it is acknowledging the higher rank of others present, dogs or people. This usually dissipates as the dog matures.

Accustom your puppy to riding in a car early. Many puppies experience car sickness on their first rides. Minimize this by withholding food before traveling, and start with short trips. For the dog's safety, confine her in a crate or specially designed car restraint when traveling. Do not allow a dog to ride in the back of a truck or hang her head out the window.

Puppy-Proofing

The big day has arrived: It is time to bring home your Poodle. Not much to think about, right? Wrong.

Like young children, puppies, even some adult dogs, are curious and mischievous, and they have a tendency to put anything and everything in their mouths. Poodle owners should puppy-proof their homes and yards to ensure the animal's safety.

Well-socialized pups grow up to be more at ease with people and other dogs.

Begin in the kitchen, because it can be such an enticing place and you tend to spend a lot of time there. Take a close look around. Are electrical cords from appliances within reach? How about breakable items that could be tugged off a counter? Store any such items well out of reach. The aroma of discarded leftovers can cause even a good dog to go bad, so be sure the garbage pail has a lid or is stored out of your Poodle's reach. Be sure your Poodle never has access to cleaning products. Consider placing safety locks on all cabinets.

Check the bathroom carefully. Store all drugs and other medicine-chest items to prevent accidental poisoning. Keep toilet bowl lids down to prevent the Poodle from drinking out of the bowl and possibly ingesting toilet bowl cleaners or other products.

Is the living room decorated with luscious green plants? Plants add life and warmth to a room, but many are poisonous. Find out which plants are pet-safe before decorating.

This shoe could have been saved if this pup had an appropriate chew toy.

Everyday household cleaners can be deadly to a curious dog. It is necessary to keep toxins and chemicals locked in cabinets and out of the dog's reach.

Are cords to the television, VCR or stereo neatly coiled and stored so the dog will not be tempted to play with them? Too often pets chew on electric cords with shocking results.

The garage is often a deadly place for pets because it is a common area to store toxic chemicals. It is essential to store toxins, such as paint and antifreeze, out of reach and to prohibit the dog from entering the garage.

The yard or kennel area must be safe, too. Make sure all fencing is secure and free of sharp edges. Do not store equipment, landscaping tools and so forth in a yard designated for the dog. Remember that anything placed in the yard is likely to be investigated.

A Dog's Second Best Friend

The benefits of regular visits to the veterinarian build trust, understanding and respect between the vet and the Poodle owner. Should an emergency or difficult situation arise, the good rapport between client and vet can make all the difference.

Basic Supplies

A certain amount of basic equipment and supplies go along with owning a dog. This means a trip to a pet supply store is in order *before* bringing home the new Poodle.

First, determine where, and in or on what, the dog will sleep. It is a good idea to assign one specific location to the dog, a "den" of sorts, to give her a sense of security. Bedding can be as simple as a blanket tossed on the floor or as elaborate as a wicker basket with a 5-inch-thick colorful print cushion. It can also be a crate, an enclosed cage with a door that is commonly used for transporting dogs on airlines. A crate is a good choice if a specific room, such as a laundry room, is not available to designate to the dog.

Now that the Poodle's bedding is squared away, consider feeding dishes. There are lots to choose from: bowls designed to keep ants out, bowls that sit in a stand and bowls made of stainless steel. Some bowls are plastic; others are earthenware. There are light bowls and heavy bowls. A case can be made for any one of these, but it is probably best to start simple. Ask your breeder,

HOUSEHOLD DANGERS

Curious puppies and inquisitive dogs get into trouble not because they are bad, but simply because they want to investigate the world around them. It's our job to protect our dogs from harmful substances, like the following:

In the Garage

antifreeze

garden supplies, like snail and slug bait, pesticides, fertilizers, mouse and rat poisons

In the House

cleaners, especially pine oil

perfumes, colognes, aftershaves

medications, vitamins

office and craft supplies

electric cords

chicken or turkey bones

chocolate, onions

some house and garden plants, like ivy, oleander and poinsettia

veterinarian or a fellow Poodle owner for a suggestion. Then select two bowls, one for food and one for water, and choose a size that best fits your Poodle's size.

11

Dogs enjoy having a place of their own, and crates, like this one, provide safety and security for pets.

Don't be overwhelmed by the myriad of collars and leashes available; the choice is one of personal preference.

Naturally, those bowls must be filled, so include dog food on the shopping list. Ask the breeder what he or she has been feeding the puppy or dog. Ask for a sample or purchase the same kind, or ask a veterinarian for a recommendation. Do not be tempted to make a radical switch because this can cause digestive upset. Change foods gradually over several days, mixing in the new food with the old diet.

A collar and leash are in order. There are leather collars and leashes; nylon, rolled or flat collars; harnesses, colorful or plain. Style is an individual choice; just make sure to attach an identification tag with a current name and telephone number to the collar.

Considering the Poodle's love of play, toys are essential. Young, teething puppies especially need safe chew toys; adult dogs may be happier with a rubber ball or pull ring, though many adult dogs still enjoy a good chew. Beware of toys with small parts.

Routine grooming is a must for every Poodle, regardless of size, so add grooming supplies and equipment to the shopping list. Purchase a brush and comb; shampoo, conditioner and some type of flea-control product; nail trimmers; and ear powder and cleaner.

Additional miscellaneous items include reference materials such as magazines and books about dogs (and specifically Poodles), carpet stain and odor remover, a "poop scoop" and a baby gate.

EXERCISE

To keep healthy, every Poodle needs exercise. How much and what type depend upon the variety of Poodle. The obviously smaller Toy does not have the same requirements as the Standard. Owners must take the Poodle's size into consideration when planning a fitness schedule. The goal, no matter what size, is a properly conditioned dog.

Playing with your Poodle is one way to get in some exercise for both of you.

CHAPTER THREE

To Good Health

THE IMPORTANCE OF PREVENTIVE CARE

There are many aspects of preventive care with which Poodle owners should be familiar: Vaccinations, regular vet visits and tooth care are just some. The advantage of preventive care is that it prevents problems.

The earlier an illness is detected in the Poodle, the easier it is for the veterinarian to treat the problem. Owners can help ensure their dogs' health by being on the lookout for medical problems. All this requires is an eye for detail and a willingness to observe. Pay close attention to your Poodle—how he looks, how he acts. What is normal behavior? How does

You can help your dog maintain good health by practicing the art of preventive care. Take good care of your Poodle today, and he will be healthy tomorrow.

his coat usually look? What are his eating and sleeping patterns? Subtle changes can indicate a problem. Keep close tabs on what is normal for your Poodle, and if anything out of the ordinary develops, call the veterinarian.

Spaying and Neutering

Spaying or neutering—surgically altering the Poodle so she or he cannot reproduce—should be at the top of every owner's "To Do" list. Why?

First, every day thousands of puppies are born in the United States as a result of uncontrolled breeding. For every pet living in a happy home today, there are four pets on the street or in abusive homes suffering from starvation, exposure, neglect or mistreatment. In six years, a single female dog and her offspring can be the source of 67,000 new dogs.

When should your Poodle be spayed or neutered? Recommendations vary among vets, but 6 months of age is commonly suggested. Ask your vet what age is best for your Poodle.

Good Nutrition

Dogs that receive the appropriate nutrients daily will be healthier and stronger than those that do not. The proper balance of proteins, fats, carbohydrates, vitamins, minerals and sufficient water enables the dog to remain healthy by fighting off illness.

ADVANTAGE OF SPAYING/NEUTERING

The greatest advantage of spaying (for females) or neutering (for males) your dog is that you are guaranteed that your dog will not produce puppies. There are too many puppies already available for too few homes. There are other advantages as well.

Advantages of Spaying

No messy heats.

No "suitors" howling at your windows or waiting in your yard.

No risk of pyometra (disease of the uterus) and decreased incidences of mammary cancer.

Advantages of Neutering

Decreased incidences of fighting, but does not affect the dog's personality.

Decreased roaming in search of bitches in season.

Decreased incidences of many urogenital diseases.

PREVENTIVE CARE PAYS

Using common sense, paying attention to your dog and working with your veterinarian, you can minimize health risks and problems. Use vet-recommended flea, tick and heartworm preventive medications; feed a nutritious diet appropriate for your dog's size, age and activity level; give your dog sufficient exercise and regular grooming; train and socialize your dog; keep current on your dog's shots; and enjoy all the years you have with your friend.

Routine Checkups

Regular visits to the veterinary clinic should begin when your Poodle is a young pup and continue throughout his life. Make this a habit and it will certainly contribute to your Poodle's good health. Even if your Poodle seems perfectly healthy, a checkup once or twice a year is in order.

Well-Being

Aside from the dog's physical needs—a proper and safe shelter, nutritious diet, health care and regular exercise—the Poodle needs plenty of plain, old-fashioned love. The dog is happiest when he is part of a family, enjoying the social interactions, nurturing and play. Bringing the Poodle into the family provides him with a sense of security.

The Poodle needs mental stimulation as well, especially because the breed is so intelligent. Obedience training is an excellent way to encourage your dog to use his mind. Remember, Poodles will use their brilliant minds in some manner, so it is best to direct them in a positive way.

Signs of Illness

Spotting illness in your Poodle early will go a long way toward a positive and safe prognosis. Actually recognizing specific signs of illness can be difficult, though. Owners must be sensitive to subtle, and sometimes not-so-subtle, signs that can indicate disease. Take note of the following list and be on the lookout for any of these:

- Changes in behavior. A normally outgoing dog may appear depressed and withdrawn.

- Changes in appetite, water intake, urination or bowel movements.

- Apparent pain or sensitivity to touch.

- Dull hair coat or excessive hair loss.

Poodles are affectionate and enjoy being with their families.

- Weight loss.
- Vomiting or diarrhea.
- Blood in urine.
- Fever or runny nose and eyes.
- Swelling or lumps.
- Lethargy.
- Convulsions or choking.
- Unusual odor.
- Strained or shallow breathing.

COMMON DISEASES

Unfortunately, even with the best preventive care, the Poodle can fall ill. Infectious diseases, which are commonly spread from dog to dog via infected urine, feces or other body secretions, can wreak havoc. Following are a few of the diseases that can affect your Poodle.

Rabies

Probably one of the most well-known diseases that can affect dogs, rabies can strike any warm-blooded animal (including humans)—and is fatal. The rabies virus, which is present in an affected animal's saliva, is usually spread through a bite or open wound. The signs of the disease can be subtle at first. Normally friendly pets can become irritable and with-

YOUR PUPPY'S VACCINES

Vaccines are given to prevent your dog from getting infectious diseases like canine distemper or rabies. Vaccines are the ultimate preventive medicine: They're given before your dog ever gets the disease so as to protect him from the disease. That's why it is necessary for your dog to be vaccinated routinely. Puppy vaccines start at 8 weeks of age for the five-in-one DHLPP vaccine and are given every three to four weeks until the puppy is 16 months old. Your veterinarian will put your puppy on a proper schedule and will remind you when to bring in your dog for shots.

drawn. Shy pets may become overly friendly. Eventually, the dog becomes withdrawn and avoids light, which hurts the eyes of a rabid dog. Fever, vomiting and diarrhea are common.

Once these symptoms develop, the animal will die; there is no treatment or cure.

Since rabid animals may have a tendency to be aggressive and bite, animals suspected of having rabies should only be handled by animal control handlers or veterinarians.

Rabies is preventable with routine vaccines, and such vaccinations are required by law for domestic animals in all states in this country.

Maintaining your Poodle's health means keeping vaccinations current.

Parvovirus

Canine parvovirus is a highly contagious and devastating illness. The hardy virus is usually transmitted through contaminated feces, but it can be carried on an infected dog's feet or skin. It strikes dogs of all ages and is most serious in young puppies.

There are two main types of parvovirus. The first signs of the diarrhea-syndrome type are usually depression and lack of appetite, followed by vomiting and the characteristic bloody diarrhea. The dog appears to be in great pain, and he usually has a high fever.

The cardiac-syndrome type affects the heart muscle and is most common in young puppies. Puppies with this condition will stop nursing, whine and gasp for air. Death may occur suddenly or in a few days. Youngsters that recover can have lingering heart failure that eventually takes their life.

Veterinarians can treat dogs with parvovirus, but the outcome varies. It depends on the age of the animal and severity of the disease. Treatment may include fluid therapy, medication to stop the severe diarrhea and antibiotics to prevent or stop secondary infection.

Young puppies receive some antibody protection against the disease from their mother, but they lose it quickly and must be vaccinated to prevent the disease. In most cases, vaccinated puppies are protected against the disease.

Coronavirus

Canine coronavirus is especially devastating to young puppies, causing depression, lack of appetite, vomiting that may contain blood and characteristically yellow-orange diarrhea. The virus is transmitted through feces, urine and saliva, and the onset of symptoms is usually rapid.

Dogs suffering from coronavirus are treated similarly to those suffering from parvovirus: fluid therapy, medication to stop diarrhea and vomiting and antibiotics if necessary.

Vaccinations are available to protect puppies and dogs against the virus and are recommended especially for those dogs in frequent contact with other dogs.

Distemper

Caused by a virus, distemper is highly contagious and is most common in unvaccinated puppies aged 3 to 8 months, but older dogs are susceptible as well.

Current vaccinations will prevent distemper in dogs, and it is especially important to vaccinate bitches before breeding to ensure maternal antibodies in the pups.

Hepatitis

Infectious canine hepatitis can affect dogs of every age, but it is most severe in puppies. It primarily affects the dog's liver, kidneys and lining of the blood vessels. Highly contagious, it is transmitted through urine, feces and saliva.

This disease has several forms. In the fatal fulminating form, the dog becomes ill very suddenly, develops bloody diarrhea and dies. In the acute form, the dog develops a fever, has bloody diarrhea, vomits blood and refuses to eat. Jaundice may be present; the whites of the dog's eyes appear yellow. Dogs with a mild case are lethargic or depressed and often refuse to eat. Infectious canine hepatitis must be diagnosed and confirmed with a blood test. Ill dogs require hospitalization. Hepatitis is preventable in dogs by keeping vaccinations current.

FLEAS AND TICKS

There are so many safe, effective products available now to combat fleas and ticks that—thankfully—they are less of a problem. Prevention is key, however. Ask your veterinarian about starting your puppy on a flea/tick repellant right away. With this, regular grooming and environmental controls, your dog and your home should stay pest-free. Without this attention, you risk infesting your dog and your home, and you're in for an ugly and costly battle to clear up the problem.

Lyme Disease

Lyme disease has received a lot of press recently, with its increased incidence throughout the United States. The illness, caused by the bacteria *Borrelia burgdorferi*, is carried by ticks. It is passed along when the tick bites a victim, canine or human. (The dog cannot pass the disease to people, though.

Three types of ticks (l-r): the wood tick, brown dog tick and deer tick.

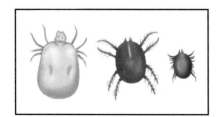

It is only transmitted via the tick.) It is most common during the tick season in May through August.

In dogs, the disease manifests itself in sudden lameness, caused by swollen joints, similar to arthritis. The dog is weak and may run a fever. The lameness can last a few days or several months, and some dogs have recurring difficulties.

Antibiotics are very effective in treating Lyme disease, and the sooner it is diagnosed and treated, the better. A vaccine is available; ask your veterinarian if your dog would benefit from it.

Kennel Cough

"Kennel cough," or the more politically correct "canine cough," shows itself as a harsh, dry cough. This contagious disease has been termed "kennel cough," much to the dismay of kennel owners, because of its often rapid spread through kennels. The cough may persist for weeks and is often followed by a bout of chronic bronchitis.

Many kennels require proof of bordatella vaccination before boarding. If your dog is in and out of kennels frequently, vaccination certainly is not a bad idea.

FIRST AID

First aid is not a substitute for professional care, though it can help save a dog's life.

To Stop Bleeding

Bleeding from a severe cut or wound must be stopped right away. There are two basic techniques—direct pressure and the tourniquet.

Try to control bleeding first by using direct pressure. Ask an assistant to hold the injured Poodle and place several pads of sterile gauze over the wound. Press. Do not wipe the wound or apply any cleansers or ointments. Apply firm, even pressure. If blood soaks through the

It is important to know the first-aid basics—just in case.

21

pad, do not remove it as this could disrupt clotting. Simply place another pad on top and continue to apply pressure.

If bleeding on a leg or the tail does not stop by applying pressure, try using a tourniquet. Use this only as a last resort. A tourniquet that is left on too long can result in limb loss.

If the dog is bleeding from his mouth or anus, or vomits or defecates blood, he may be suffering from internal injuries. Do not attempt to stop bleeding. Call the veterinarian right away for emergency treatment.

Shock

Whenever a dog is injured or is seriously ill, the odds are good that he will go into a state of shock. A decreased supply of oxygen to the tissues usually results in unconsciousness; pale gums; weak, rapid pulse; and labored, rapid breathing. If not treated, a dog will die from shock. The conditions of the dog should continue to be treated, but the dog should be as comfortable as possible. A blanket can help keep a dog warm. A dog in shock needs immediate veterinary care.

Poisoning

A dog's curiosity will often lead him to eat or lick things he shouldn't. Unfortunately, many substances are poisonous to dogs, including household products, plants or chemicals. Owners must learn to act quickly if poisoning is suspected because the results can be deadly.

If your dog appears to be poisoned:

- Call your veterinarian and follow his or her directions.

- Try to identify the poison source—this is really important. Take the container or plant to the clinic.

- Never try to induce vomiting in a semi- or unconscious animal.

- Transport the dog to the clinic as directed by the vet. Bring with

POISON ALERT

If your dog has ingested a potentially poisonous substance, waste no time. Call the National Animal Poison Control Center hot line:

(800) 548-2423 ($30 per case) or

(900) 680-0000 ($20 first five minutes; $2.95 each additional minute)

22

you the telephone number for the National Animal Poison Control Center.

Heatstroke

Heatstroke can be deadly and must be treated immediately to save the dog. Signs include rapid panting, darker-than-usual gums and tongue, salivating, exhaustion or vomiting. The dog's body temperature is elevated, sometimes as high as 106°F. If the dog is not treated, coma and death can follow.

If heatstroke is suspected, cool down your overheated dog as quickly as possible. Mildly affected dogs can be moved to a cooler environment, into an air-conditioned home, for example, or wrapped in moistened towels. Call your veterinarian.

Insect Bites/Stings

Just like people, dogs can suffer bee stings and insect bites. Bees, wasps and yellow jackets leave a nasty, painful sting; and if your dog is stung repeatedly, shock can occur.

If an insect bite is suspected, try to identify the culprit. Remove the stinger if it is a bee sting, and apply a mixture of baking soda and water

to the sting. It is also a good idea to apply ice packs to reduce inflammation and ease pain. Call your veterinarian, especially if your dog seems ill or goes into shock.

INTERNAL PARASITES

Dogs are susceptible to several internal parasites. Keeping your Poodle free of internal parasites is another important aspect of health care. Watch for general signs of poor condition: a dull coat, weight loss, lethargy, coughing, weakness and diarrhea.

For proper diagnosis and treatment of internal parasites, consult a veterinarian.

Regular veterinary checkups, daily exercise, balanced nutrition and a lot of old-fashioned TLC will help keep your Poodle happy and healthy.

23

WHEN TO CALL THE VETERINARIAN

In any emergency situation, you should call your veterinarian immediately. Try to stay calm when you call, and give the vet or the assistant as much information as possible before you leave for the clinic. That way, the staff will be able to take immediate, specific action when you arrive. Emergencies include:

- Bleeding or deep wounds
- Hyperthermia (overheating)
- Shock
- Dehydration
- Abdominal pain
- Burns
- Fits
- Unconsciousness
- Broken bones
- Paralysis

Call your veterinarian if you suspect any health troubles.

Roundworms

Roundworms, or ascarids, are probably the most common worms that affect dogs. Most puppies are born with these organisms in their intestines, which is why youngsters are treated for these parasites as soon as it is safe to do so.

Animals contract roundworms by ingesting infected soil and feces. A roundworm infestation can rob vital nutrients from young puppies and cause diarrhea, vomiting and digestive upset. Roundworms can also harm a young animal's liver and lungs, so treatment is imperative.

Tapeworms

Tapeworms are commonly transmitted by fleas to dogs. Tapeworm eggs enter the body of a canine host when the animal accidentally ingests a carrier flea. The parasite settles in the intestines, where it sinks its head into the intestinal wall and feeds off material the host is digesting. The worm grows a body of egg packets, which break off periodically and are expelled from the body in the feces. Fleas then ingest the eggs from the feces, and the parasite's life cycle begins all over again.

Hookworms

Hookworms are so named because they hook onto an animal's small intestine and suck the host's blood.

Like roundworms, hookworms are contracted when a dog ingests contaminated soil or feces.

Hookworms can be especially devastating to dogs. They will become thin and sick; puppies can die. An affected dog will suffer from bloody diarrhea and, if the parasites migrate to the lungs, the dog may contract bronchitis or pneumonia.

Hookworms commonly strike puppies 2 to 8 weeks of age and are less common in adult dogs.

Whipworms

Known for their threadlike appearance, whipworms attach into the wall of the large intestine to feed. Thick-shelled eggs are passed in the feces and in about two to four weeks are mature and able to reinfect a host that ingests the eggs.

Mild whipworm infestation is often without signs, but as the worms grow, weight loss, bloody diarrhea and anemia follow. In areas where the soil is heavily contaminated, frequent checks are advised to prevent severe infestation.

Heartworms

Heartworms larvae are transmitted by the ordinary mosquito, but the effects are far from ordinary. In three to four months, the larvae (microfilaria) become small worms and make their way to a vein, where they are transported to the heart, where they grow and reproduce.

At first, a dog with heartworms is free of symptoms. The signs vary, but the most common is a deep cough and shortness of breath. The dog tires easily, is weak and loses weight. Eventually, the dog may suffer from congestive heart failure.

EXTERNAL PARASITES

FLEAS—Besides carrying tapeworm larvae, fleas bite and suck the host's blood. Their bites itch and are extremely annoying to dogs, especially if the dog is hypersensitive to the bite. Fleas must be eliminated on the dog with special shampoos and dips. Fleas also infest the dog's bedding and the owner's home and yard.

TICKS—Several varieties of ticks attach themselves to dogs, where they burrow into the skin and suck blood. Ticks can be carriers of several diseases, including Lyme disease and Rocky Mountain Spotted Fever.

WHAT'S WRONG WITH MY DOG?

We've listed some common symptoms of health problems and their possible causes. If any of the following symptoms appear serious immediately or persist for more than 24 hours, make an appointment to see your veterinarian immediately.

CONDITIONS	POSSIBLE CAUSES
DIARRHEA	Intestinal upset, typically caused by eating something bad or overeating. Can also be a viral infection, a bad case of nerves or anxiety or a parasite infection. If you see blood in the feces, get to the vet right away.
VOMITING/RETCHING	Dogs regurgitate fairly regularly (bitches for their young), whenever something upsets their stomachs, or even out of excitement or anxiety. Often dogs eat grass, which, because it's indigestible in its pure form, irritates their stomachs and causes them to vomit. Getting a good look at *what* your dog vomited can better indicate what's causing it.
COUGHING	Obstruction in the throat; virus (kennel cough); roundworm infestation; congestive heart failure.
RUNNY NOSE	Because dogs don't catch colds like people, a runny nose is a sign of congestion or irritation.
LOSS OF APPETITE	Because most dogs are hearty and regular eaters, a loss of appetite can be your first and most accurate sign of a serious problem.
LOSS OF ENERGY (LETHARGY)	Any number of things could be slowing down your dog, from an infection to internal tumors to overexercise—even overeating.

LICE—Lice are not common in dogs, but when they are present they cause intense irritation and itching. There are two types: biting and sucking. Biting lice feed on skin scales, and sucking lice feed on blood.

MITES—There are several types of mites that cause several kinds of mange, including sarcoptic, demodectic and cheyletiella. These microscopic mites cause intense itching and misery to the dog.

CONDITIONS	POSSIBLE CAUSES
STINKY BREATH	Imagine if you never brushed your teeth! Foul-smelling breath indicates plaque and tartar buildup that could possibly have caused infection. Start brushing your dog's teeth.
LIMPING	This could be caused by something as simple as a hurt or bruised pad, to something as complicated as hip dysplasia, torn ligaments or broken bones.
CONSTANT ITCHING	Probably due to fleas, mites or an allergic reaction to food or environment (your vet will need to help you determine what your dog's allergic to).
RED, INFLAMED ITCHY SPOTS	Often referred to as "hot spots," these are particularly common on coated breeds. They're caused by a bacterial infection that gets aggravated as the dog licks and bites at the spot.
BALD SPOTS	These are the result of excessive itching or biting at the skin so that the hair follicles are damaged; excessively dry skin; mange; calluses; and even infections. You need to determine what the underlying cause is.
STINKY EARS/HEADSHAKING	Take a look under your dog's ear flap. Do you see brown, waxy buildup? Clean the ears with something soft and a special cleaner, and don't use cotton swabs or go too deep into the ear canal.
UNUSUAL LUMPS	Could be fatty tissue, could be something serious (infection, trauma, tumor). Don't wait to find out.

27

GENETIC PREDISPOSITIONS

Hip Dysplasia

Hip dysplasia is most common in Standard Poodles. The hips undergo progressive structural changes, eventually leading to lameness. The first signs of the problem are joint laxity, followed by abnormal gait, stiffness and lameness. It can be severely crippling.

External parasites, intense heat and insect bites and stings can threaten your Poodle.

28

Diagnosis is made by taking x-rays and examining the hips for changes, including erosion of the joints, subluxation and arthritic changes.

Responsible Poodle breeders, especially Standard breeders, screen for hip dysplasia. Those considering purchasing a Standard puppy should make sure the parents and grandparents have been tested by the Orthopedic Foundation for Animals. This is almost a guarantee that the dog will not develop hip dysplasia, but there is always the chance the problem may arise.

Progressive Retinal Atrophy

Progressive retinal atrophy (PRA) is found in all sizes but is most common in the smaller Poodles. PRA causes the retina to degenerate gradually and eventually leads to blindness. It usually comes on late, when the dog is 5 to 7 years old.

The Canine Eye Registration Foundation (CERF) "certifies" dogs free of eye disease, including PRA, and collects research on canine eye disease. Again, reputable breeders routinely screen for PRA and certify their dogs free of the condition.

Congenital Epilepsy

Epilepsy is a recurrent seizure disorder, causing seizures, "fits" or convulsions. Affected dogs may jerk uncontrollably, foam at the mouth, collapse and lose normal consciousness. Seizures are caused by a burst of electrical activity in the brain. While there is no cure for the condition, it can be controlled somewhat successfully with medication.

29

CHAPTER FOUR

Positively Nutritious

Well, thanks to commercially prepared foods, owners need not scientifically calculate and formulate a pet's meal. Feeding a nutritionally balanced diet can be as easy—and complete—as opening a bag or can of food. Such foods have been prepared by companies dedicated to understanding the nutritional needs of dogs.

Food. It's the fuel the Poodle needs to nourish her body, which, in turn, produces that special kind of Poodle energy owners so appreciate and enjoy.

The domestic dog requires some forty-five to fifty different nutrients in her diet. A deficiency of any one of those nutrients can cause illness.

To prevent any such problems, an owner must make sure the Poodle eats properly and takes in the appropriate balance of nutrients. Easier said than done, right?

NUTRITION

PROTEIN—The Poodle relies on specific nutrients for its vigorous health and spectacular coat. Proteins, which are composed of amino acids found in meats, eggs, fish and soybeans, supply dogs with nutrients needed for growth, tissue repair and maintenance. They also form antibodies to fight infection.

CARBOHYDRATES—Carbohydrates are the Poodle's energy sources. The dog's body uses carbohydrates for quick energy, thus sparing protein for body growth and repair. Cellulose, an indigestible carbohydrate, provides bulk for proper intestinal function.

FATS—Fats provide the Poodle with the most concentrated source of energy. They carry fat-soluble vitamins—D, E, A and K—and supply linoleic acid, a fatty acid that is important for skin and hair.

VITAMINS AND MINERALS—Vitamins and minerals are essential for normal body functions and bone development, as well as for certain chemical reactions in the body. For example, zinc is a trace mineral required for normal metabolism, including hair growth and skin health. A deficiency of zinc in a dog's diet can cause thinning hair and crusty dermatitis. And a deficiency of essential fatty acids can retard growth and produce coarse hair and dry, flaking skin.

WATER—Last, but by no means least, is water. Dogs need a constant supply of fresh, clean water.

Selecting Food

Finding the best diet for an individual dog may take some detective work. Ask the breeder for a recommendation. An experienced breeder usually has experimented with a number of brands of food, knows which foods agree with his or her Poodles and can give an unbiased opinion. Ask a veterinarian or pet supply retailer for a suggestion. Ask other Poodle owners for ideas. Then pick one and give it a try.

A good way to evaluate how a specific food agrees with your

Bright eyes, healthy coat and sufficient energy indicate that a Poodle is eating a well-balanced diet.

GROWTH STAGE OF FOODS

Once upon a time, there was puppy food and there was adult dog food. Now there are foods for puppies, young adults/active dogs, less active dogs and senior citizens. What's the difference between these foods? They vary by the amounts of nutrients they provide for the dog's growth stage/activity level.

Less active dogs don't need as much protein or fat as growing, active dogs; senior dogs don't need some of the nutrients vital to puppies. By feeding a high-quality food that's appropriate for your dog's age and activity level, you're benefiting your dog and yourself. Feed too much protein to a couch potato and she'll have energy to spare, which means a few more trips around the block will be needed to burn it off. Feed an adult diet to a puppy, and risk growth and development abnormalities that could affect her for a lifetime.

If your Poodle eats all of her food at mealtime and seems to be healthy, chances are you are feeding properly.

Poodle is to evaluate the feces on a regular basis. While certainly not a pleasant task, it is important. Most healthy dogs leave well-formed, firm droppings that emit little odor. Diarrhea is obviously a sign of illness, as is any other sudden change in the feces consistency. Such changes can also indicate a poor diet.

Types of Food

There are three basic types of commercial dog food: dry, canned and semimoist. Which one is best for the Poodle? For the most part, all diets have their advantages.

One of the biggest differences between dry and canned foods is moisture content. Obviously, the moisture content in canned food is higher: 70 to 80 percent. Dry food is around 10 percent. Canned food is usually manufactured from fresh meat products, which accounts for the added moisture.

This higher moisture content has both an advantage and disadvantage. It is very appealing to dogs, but it is more expensive than the other varieties. The price per ounce of dry and canned food is about the same, but owners must feed three times as much canned food to meet caloric requirements. For large breeds, the costs can be prohibitive. Some say canned food is more digestible and that it has a longer shelf life because cans are sealed airtight.

A complete and balanced dry food is usually the most economical. It also helps eliminate tartar buildup on the dog's teeth and gums. Dry food must be stored properly to ensure its nutritional value, and the shelf life is an estimated twelve months. Most dry foods contain approved chemical preservatives such as BHA, BHT and ethoxyquin.

Dry food can seem boring to owners, which accounts for the practice of mixing a small portion of canned with dry food. Feeding a dry diet by itself, as long as the diet is "complete and balanced," is perfectly sufficient.

TO SUPPLEMENT OR NOT TO SUPPLEMENT

If you're feeding your dog a diet that's correct for her developmental stage and she's alert, healthy-looking and neither over- nor underweight, you don't need to add supplements. These include table scraps as well as vitamins and minerals. In fact, unless you are a nutrition expert, using food supplements can actually hurt a growing puppy. For example, mixing too much calcium into your dog's food can lead to musculoskeletal disorders. Educating yourself about the quantity of vitamins your dog needs to be healthy will help you determine what needs to be supplemented. If you have any concerns about the nutritional quality of the food you're feeding, discuss them with your veterinarian.

In between dry and canned foods are semimoist diets. These processed diets are usually packaged

33

Rapidly growing, energetic puppies require a higher caloric intake and need to eat more frequently than adult dogs.

HOW MANY MEALS A DAY?

Individual dogs vary in how much they should eat to maintain a desired body weight—not too fat, but not too thin. Puppies need several meals a day, while older dogs may need only one. Determine how much food keeps your adult dog looking and feeling her best. Then decide how many meals you want to feed with that amount. Like us, most dogs love to eat, and offering two meals a day is more enjoyable for them. If you're worried about overfeeding, make sure you measure correctly and abstain from adding tidbits to the meals.

Whether you feed one or two meals, only leave your dog's food out for the amount of time it takes her to eat it—ten minutes, for example. Free-feeding (when food is available any time) and leisurely meals encourage picky eating. Don't worry if your dog doesn't finish all her dinner in the allotted time. She'll learn she should.

conveniently, eliminating the mess of canned food or the bulk of a 25-pound bag. Costs fall between canned and dry food, but shelf life is somewhat less than either.

It is best to avoid diets with high amounts of sugar, dyes or preservatives.

Today, Poodles enjoy the benefits of diets made specifically for differing stages in life: puppy diets, adult diets and diets for seniors. Such diets are made with the dog's specific caloric needs in mind. There are also special diets made for dogs with health problems. Ask your veterinarian if a special diet is appropriate for your Poodle before feeding one.

How Much?

How much to feed your Poodle will vary among individual dogs depending upon size, activity, temperament, environment and metabolism. While it's obvious that a Standard Poodle will need more food than a Toy, it's not so clear how much your Standard (or Toy) should eat compared to someone else's. Again, your dog's breeder, fellow Poodle owners and your own common sense can help you determine how much is enough for your dog.

Given that weight can vary, you should examine your dog to see if the body fat is in correct proportion to height and bone. There should be a layer of subcutaneous fat over the ribs, thick enough to provide some padding and insulation, but not too thick. Individual ribs should be evident to the touch.

Feeding Frequency

How often the Poodle needs to eat varies throughout her life, and varies among individual dogs.

Young puppies need to eat frequently. Generally, you should feed them four times daily at 6 to 8 weeks of age, and three times daily by 10 to 12 weeks. Once the puppy reaches 16 weeks (4 months) twice a day is sufficient. As the puppy becomes less interested in finishing a meal or becomes overweight, eliminate a feeding. At 1 year of age, one feeding a day is adequate. Breaking up the dog's daily allotment into two feedings, however, is generally more pleasant for the dog.

Some owners "free-feed," which means they fill up the bowl and leave it out. This is not recommended because it sends the message that the dog can eat at any time. It will also make it more difficult for you to know when your dog's not feeling 100 percent, as missing a meal is often the first sign.

Obesity

There is a great temptation for owners of all varieties of Poodles to overfeed. Overfeeding and obesity go hand in hand, however.

If you are worried about overfeeding, avoid feeding your dog table scraps and excess treats.

Unfortunately, it is the dog that suffers: An overweight dog is uncomfortable, lethargic and prone to heart disease and other illnesses.

FOOD ALLERGIES

If your puppy or dog seems to itch all the time for no apparent reason, she could be allergic to one or more ingredients in her food. This is not uncommon, and it's why many foods contain lamb and rice instead of beef, wheat or soy. Have your dog tested by your veterinarian, and be patient while you strive to identify and eliminate the allergens from your dog's food (or environment).

35

Types of Food/Treats

There are three types of commercially available dog food—dry, canned and semimoist—and a huge assortment of treats (lucky dogs!) to feed your dog. Which should you choose?

Dry and canned foods contain similar ingredients. The primary difference between them is their moisture content. The moisture is not just water. It's blood and broth, too, the very things that dogs adore. So while canned food is more palatable, dry food is more economical, convenient and effective in controlling tartar buildup. Most owners feed a 25 percent canned/75 percent dry diet to give their dogs the benefit of both. Just be sure your dog is getting the nutrition she needs (you and your veterinarian can determine this).

Semimoist foods have the flavor dogs love and the convenience owners want. However, they tend to contain excessive amounts of artificial colors and preservatives.

Dog treats come in every size, shape and flavor imaginable, from organic cookies shaped like postmen to beefy chew sticks. Dogs seem to love them all, so enjoy the variety. Just be sure not to overindulge your dog. Factor treats into her regular meal sizes.

Foods to Avoid

Chocolate, with a chemical ingredient called theobromine, can cause severe digestive upset and even death. Keep all chocolate, especially the kind used for baking, which has the highest amount of theobromine, away from the dog.

Rich foods, such as turkey skin, gravy and mashed potatoes, are popular around the holiday season, but don't allow your dog to indulge in them. The high fat content of such food will cause digestive upset.

Spicy foods are a no-no for the Poodle as well. Don't add raw eggs to the dog's food, either. Raw eggs can contain the potentially deadly bacteria salmonella.

Bones

Dogs love to chew bones, but not all bones are safe for dogs. Avoid giving the Poodle turkey, chicken or pork bones—they can splinter and cause intestinal damage. Large, hard and round bones, such as knuckle or marrowbones, are better choices. Parboil the bone to kill bacteria before offering it to your dog. Make sure the dog only chews the bone. Take it away if she begins to eat it.

Better yet, purchase chew toys. There are many safe and well-made synthetic bones on the market that will satisfy the dog's urge to chew.

CHAPTER FIVE

Putting on the Dog

The Poodle's wonderful temperament has a purpose. This good-natured dog makes an excellent friend for adults and children, a top hunting companion and an incredible showman. But what may be of greater importance is that the Poodle really enjoys grooming, which is fortunate considering the amount of time and money required to keep a coat in good shape, whether he be pet or show dog. Some people get a Poodle because the breed doesn't shed, which is nice for housecleaning and for people with allergies to dog hair and dandruff. However, while they don't shed, their coats do grow quickly, and they need regular grooming.

Poodles are often favorite customers of professional groomers because they can be taught to sit or stand quietly for brushing or scissoring, hold a paw up for clipping or peacefully tolerate ear cleaning. Poodles are blessed with spectacular coats, and a freshly bathed, fluffed and trimmed Poodle is a beautiful sight.

Poodles are known to actually love the grooming process—good thing, since they all need it.

Poodle grooming is an art form, and it requires skill, talent, patience, equipment and know-how. This is not to suggest that owners cannot learn to trim their own Poodles. They can. The reality is, however, that most owners do not learn the skill; instead, they ask a professional groomer to do the job.

Of course, owners must pay groomers for such services—again and again and again. Pet Poodles require full grooming—bath, fluff dry and hair cut—at least every six to eight weeks. In between visits, Poodles must be brushed and

sometimes bathed, ears and teeth must be checked weekly and toenails may need to be trimmed or filed.

The grooming information here is geared to what owners can do for their pet Poodles at home.

SELECTING A BRUSH

Brushing and combing are the foundations of good grooming. It is essential to master these skills. Neglect brushing and combing, and your Poodle will look like a tattered coat.

The type of brush you use depends on the dog's coat and whether it is being groomed for show or home. The best is a wire slicker or pin brush. The wire slicker is excellent for brushing the thick, dense parts of the coat and for brushing out tangles. A pin brush is less effective on tangled coats, but it is excellent for the Poodle's long, silky ears and other long parts of the coat. Used properly, a pin brush will not tear or damage the coat as much as a slicker brush.

Opinions do vary among groomers and Poodle breeders as to which brush is best. Ask your dog's breeder or a groomer what type of brush he or she uses.

TECHNIQUE

Where do you begin once you have selected a brush? Assuming that the Poodle is well-mannered and famil- iar with the grooming process, place him on the grooming table. If a grooming table is not available, try the kitchen counter, washing machine, picnic table or any location that is waist high and easy to clean. Be sure to place a rubber mat beneath the dog on slippery surfaces such as a countertop. You should groom the Poodle in this selected spot each time. That way, the dog will know what to expect at each grooming session.

Brushing, and the entire groom- ing process, should be a systematic procedure. Many professional groomers begin brushing the dog's hindquarters, move to the hind legs, tail, front legs, body and finally the head and ears. When brushing is done systematically, it takes less time to brush the coat completely. The important idea is to develop a brushing pattern and use it each time.

A thorough brushing must pre- cede bathing. This is especially important if the coat is long and/or thick. Soaking a tangled coat with

Poodles are high- maintenance dogs, though they are well worth the effort.

water will only tighten the tangles, making them difficult, if not impos- sible, to remove. It is tempting to wash a dirty Poodle first, then

GROOMING TOOLS

pin brush	scissors
slicker brush	nail clippers
flea comb	tooth-cleaning equipment
towel	shampoo
mat rake	conditioner
grooming glove	clippers

Light-skinned Poodles are most susceptible to brush-burn, so be sure to brush the coat without brushing the skin.

Metal combs are most durable and easy to clean.

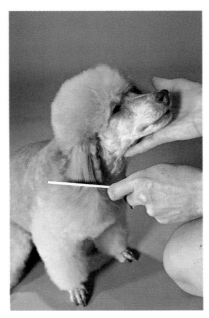

brush. Don't. It just creates a bigger brushing job.

Brushing the Poodle correctly can be tricky, because there is usually so much to brush. It is important to brush down to the skin, without actually brushing the skin. This can be accomplished by pushing back, or parting, the coat with one hand and brushing the hair down a little at a time with the other. Use quick, deep strokes of the brush, and brush small areas. Do not rake the brush over the dog's skin. This will cause a condition known as brush-burn, in which the skin becomes red, irritated and uncomfortable. Pink- and light-skinned Poodles seem to be more sensitive to this.

Should the Poodle stand, sit or lie down while being brushed? That is really a personal preference. Choose whichever is easiest.

Combing should follow brushing. Once the Poodle is brushed thoroughly, run a comb through his locks to detect snarls missed by brushing. The comb is the perfect tool for finishing touches, such as smoothing or fluffing the coat.

What type of comb is best? There are many styles of combs from which to choose, but the most durable and easy-to-clean combs are metal, either with or without a handle. For everyday purposes, a medium-tooth width is best. A fine-tooth "flea" comb should be used only for combing out fleas.

CLIPPING NAILS

While the dog is standing, look to see if the nails touch the table. If they do, they probably need trimming. The idea is to keep the nails trimmed so they do not touch the ground—and you do not hear that telltale click-click down the hallway.

To trim the nails, hold a paw firmly in one hand. Place your thumb on top of the foot and fingers underneath to spread the toes. With the clippers in your other hand, clip the very tips of the nails, one at a time, with short, decisive strokes. Do not forget the dewclaws, which appear at wrist level.

If you cut the nail too short (or if the quick has grown out too long) the Poodle will yelp and pull back, and the nail will start to bleed. Try not to panic. Simply drop the clippers—keeping hold of the paw—and grab a pinch of styptic powder between your thumb and forefinger. Apply this to the bleeding nail and press. Hold it for thirty

Nails should be trimmed short enough that they do not touch the ground.

41

This Poodle's nails are in need of a trim.

seconds or so. Continue until the bleeding stops.

File the nails on the first paw before moving on to the next paw. A few swipes of the file will usually remove any rough edges.

EYES AND EARS

Is there a bright sparkle in your Poodle's eyes? If so, they are probably healthy, and all you need to do is gently wipe the corners with a water-moistened cotton ball. It is not a good idea to use eyedrops or other eye ointments unless they are prescribed by a veterinarian. If you notice redness, cloudiness, excessive tearing or inflammation, call your veterinarian right away.

Ear care is more involved. Look inside the Poodle's ears. Healthy ears are clean, free of debris and without odor. Chances are there is hair growing in the Poodle's ear canal. This is normal for this breed, but it should be removed to help prevent infection and to make the ears easier to clean. (Opinions do vary as to whether or not the ear hair should be removed. Ask your vet what is best for your Poodle.)

Generally, the Poodle's healthy ears will not need a lot of cleaning.

Wipe them out with a dry cotton ball or one slightly moistened with mineral oil each time you groom. There are many commercially prepared ear cleaners, though it may not be necessary to use one if the ears are clean. Ask your vet which cleaner, if any, is best for your Poodle.

HEALTHY TEETH

Examine your Poodle's teeth and gums for signs of disease. Are the gums inflamed? Are the teeth marred with tartar buildup? Does the dog's breath smell bad? Call the vet with questions regarding any of these suspicious symptoms.

Should you brush your Poodle's teeth? Absolutely! By beginning during puppyhood, the Poodle will accept the procedure quite well. Purchase a "doggie" toothbrush and toothpaste at a pet-supply store, then brush approximately once a week.

Never use human toothpaste to brush your Poodle's teeth. It can cause severe digestive upset. Use only toothpaste formulated for dogs.

THE BATH

It may seem odd that bathing is last on the grooming list, but it is for good reason. The coat must be brushed first or bathing will tighten the tangles, and styptic and ear powders are messy. Bathing enables you to cleanse a mat-free coat and remove powders.

Once your dog is secured in the tub, place a cotton ball in each ear to keep water out. Saturate the dog with warm water, beginning at the top of the head. Work back, soaking the top of the head and the ears (do not spray directly in the dog's face or ears) and moving along the back to the tail. Begin at the head again, this time underneath the chin, to the neck, chest and front legs. Then soak the sides, stomach, rear end and, finally, the back legs. Be sure the dog is wet to the skin. It may take several moments of soaking to get through the Poodle's dense coat. Remember, this breed was originally bred to work in water and has the coat to prove it!

Apply shampoo, beginning with the head and working down the back to the tail. Take care not to get soap in the dog's eyes. Many groomers dilute shampoo in a plastic bucket and apply it with a sponge.

Once the dog is soapy, start scrubbing, literally. Massage the soap into the fur with your hands. Use the

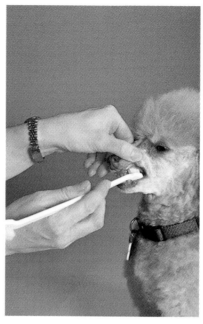

Prevent bad doggy breath by brushing your Poodle's teeth once a week.

43

sponge to clean the stomach and genital areas. Rinse well, again beginning with the head and working down the back to the tail, then repeat the process.

The final rinse is especially important because soap left in the dog's coat will irritate his skin and look like flakes of dandruff. Once you think you have rinsed all the soap out, rinse again.

Towel dry the dog while he is secured in the tub. It may take several towels to absorb the excess water, so be sure to have them handy before bathing.

FLUFF DRYING

Fluff drying is, for the most part, the secret to giving the Poodle a smooth, fluffed look. Because the coat is naturally curly, it will, when left to dry on its own, dry curly. Fluff drying—drying while brushing continuously—straightens and fluffs the coat. A fluff-dried coat looks beautiful and is easier to scissor and shape.

Fluff drying is by no means an easy task. It's tricky to learn how to brush dry the coat a little bit at a time before the rest of the coat dries on its own—curly.

Those willing to give it a try first need a few supplies: a soft slicker brush and a blow dryer, preferably one on a stand to leave both arms free. As with brushing, drying must be done systematically. Groomers all have different ideas about where to begin, but here is one plan of action:

STEP 1—Fluff dry the top knot and ears. Keep a towel wrapped around the Poodle's body while you are doing this to keep the body coat from curling.

STEP 2—Fluff dry the neck, chest and front legs, one at a time. Keep the towel wrapped around the middle and hindquarters.

STEP 3—Fluff dry the tail pom, rear and back legs, one at a time.

STEP 4—Fluff the remaining body area and stomach.

For the fluffed look, try blow-drying the Poodle's top knot and ears before the rest of its body.

These steps will vary according to your dog's coat length and trim style. The idea is to fluff each part of the coat before it dries on its own.

The technique for fluff drying can be tricky, as well. Aim the dryer at one area, the top knot for example. Brush quickly and softly until the hair is completely dry. Be careful not to brush too hard; that will irritate the dog's skin. Once the top knot is dry, aim the dryer at one of the ears and begin drying, a few

44

strands at a time. Brush constantly. Continue on to the rest of the coat. If the coat dries before you can fluff it, dampen it with water.

A WORD ABOUT TRIMS

Every Poodle, whether pet or show dog, must be trimmed. Some pet owners groom their Poodles; many use the services of a professional groomer. Styles for pet Poodles mirror those in the show ring, with a variety as numerous as the colors in the rainbow. You must decide who will trim your Poodle and in what style.

If you are thinking of trimming your dog, you must be very determined—and skilled.

Before deciding to trim your Poodle, consider the following:

- the cost of equipment, including electric clippers, blades and scissors

- the danger of scissors in unskilled hands

- the challenge of trimming a wiggly puppy or dog

- the years of practice required to perfect trimming skills

Styles for your pet Poodle are really a matter of personal preference. Some owners like simple utility trims; others like elaborate patterns. To get an idea of the many trims available, read grooming books (there are many good ones dedicated to grooming the Poodle), visit grooming shops or talk with other Poodle owners.

SELECTING A GROOMER

Fortunately, there are many skilled and kind professional groomers. But how do you choose one?

Ask your breeder, veterinarian or a fellow Poodle owner for a recommendation. Look through the telephone directory; pick several to call and visit (without the dog).

Meet with the groomer. Take note of her professionalism. Is she certified? (There are many excellent groomers who are not certified, but the industry is leaning toward man-datory certification.) Does she seem to genuinely love animals? Is she fa-miliar with a variety of Poodle trims? Is she easy to communicate with? Is the shop clean?

45

The "English saddle trim" modeled by this white Miniature is extremely versatile and can be styled in many ways.

This white Standard sports a puppy clip.

Is the pricing fair? Pay attention to first impressions.

After visiting a few shops, pick one. Next, make an appointment. Be sure to communicate clearly how you want the dog trimmed. If you're not sure, ask the groomer for ideas or suggestions.

A groomer is definitely one of your Poodle's best friends. Select one carefully.

CHAPTER SIX

Measuring Up

*N o dog surpasses the Poodle in intel-
ligence; in fact, no dog is her equal.
She has a quality of mind that bor-
ders on the human; her reasoning pow-
ers are evident to all with whom she is
associated, and there is apparently no
limit to her aptitude for learning.*

William A. Bruette
The AKC Complete Dog Book

What exactly is a Poodle? How do
we know what a Poodle should look
like? How should it act? What about
size and color? How does it differ
from other breeds of dogs?

To find the answers to these
questions, we look to what is called
a "breed standard."

The breed standard is an important reference point for dog breeders

because it gives an overall picture. By
outlining the specifics of a particular
breed of dog, breeders nationwide are
able to strive toward one goal, though
interpretations may vary. This allows
for consistency within the breed and
for dogs that reflect the best of a
breed.

Follow along with a look at the
Official Standard for the Poodle,
which was approved by the American
Kennel Club on August 14, 1984,
and reformatted March 27, 1990, by
the Poodle Club of America. This is
where we look to truly understand

The Standard Poodle is believed to be the oldest among today's three sizes.

the Poodle, at least in the literal sense. You will find that some understanding of the Poodle is subjective, and you will have to learn this through living and sharing a home with the dog. In the following discussion, the sections in italics are taken directly from the standard; the rest is commentary.

GENERAL APPEARANCE, CARRIAGE AND CONDITION

The Poodle today, according to the breed standard, *is a very active, intelligent and elegant-appearing dog, squarely built, well proportioned,* *moving soundly and carrying herself proudly. Properly clipped in the traditional fashion and carefully groomed, the Poodle has about her an air of distinction and dignity peculiar to herself.*

Size, Proportion, Substance

SIZE

The Standard, Miniature and Toy Poodles are not separate breeds. Rather, they are the three different sizes of one breed.

The Standard Poodle is over 15 inches at the highest point of the shoulders. Any Poodle which is 15 inches or less in height shall be disqualified from competition as a Standard Poodle.

The Miniature Poodle is 15 inches or under at the highest point of the shoulders, with a minimum height in excess of 10 inches. Any Poodle which is over 15 inches or is 10 or less at the highest point of the shoulders shall be disqualified from competition as a Miniature Poodle.

The Toy Poodle is 10 inches or under at the highest point of the shoulders. Any Poodle which is more than 10 inches at the highest point of the shoulders shall be disqualified from competition as a Toy Poodle.

PROPORTION

To insure the desirable squarely built appearance, the length of body measured from the breastbone to the point of the rump approximates the height from the highest point of the shoulders to the ground.

SUBSTANCE

Bone and muscle of both forelegs and hindlegs are in proportion to size of dog.

Head and Expression

The Poodle's eyes *are very dark, oval in shape and set far enough apart and positioned to create an alert, intelligent expression. Major fault: eyes round, protruding, large or very light.*

The ears *should be hanging close to the head, set at or slightly below eye level. The ear leather is long, wide and thickly feathered; however, the ear fringe should not be of excessive length.*

The Poodle's skull *is moderately rounded, with a slight but definite stop. Cheekbones and muscles flat. Length from occiput to stop about the same as length of muzzle.*

The muzzle *is long, straight and fine, with slight chiseling under the eyes. Strong without lippiness. The chin definite enough to preclude snipiness. Major fault: lack of chin.*

WHAT IS A BREED STANDARD?

A breed standard—a detailed description of an individual breed—is meant to portray the ideal specimen of that breed. This includes ideal structure, temperament, gait, type—all aspects of the dog. Because the standard describes an ideal specimen, it isn't based on any particular dog. It is a concept against which judges compare actual dogs and breeders strive to produce dogs. At a dog show, the dog that wins is the one that comes closest, in the judge's opinion, to the standard for its breed. Breed standards are written by the breed parent clubs, the national organizations formed to oversee the well-being of the breed. They are voted on and approved by the members of the parent clubs.

49

Historians have theorized that Miniatures are the result of breeding small Standards.

and muscular. The tail is straight, set on high and carried up, docked of sufficient length to insure a balanced outline. *Major fault: set low, curled or carried over the back.*

Forequarters

The Poodle should have *strong, smoothly muscled shoulders. The shoulder blade is well laid back and approximately the same length as the upper foreleg. Major fault: steep shoulder.*

The forelegs are *straight and parallel when viewed from the front. When viewed from the side the elbow is directly below the highest point of the shoulder. The pasterns are strong. Dewclaws may be removed.*

The feet are *rather small, oval in shape with toes well arched and cushioned on thick firm pads. Nails short but not excessively shortened. The feet turn neither in nor out. Major fault: paper or splay foot.*

Hindquarters

The angulation of the hindquarters balances that of the forequarters. Hind legs straight and parallel when viewed from the rear. Muscular with width in the region of the stifles, which are

Toy Poodles are said to be the result of breeding small Miniatures. These tiny dogs are probably the most pampered of all the sizes.

The teeth are *white, strong and with a scissors bite. Major fault: undershot, overshot, wry mouth.*

Neck, Topline, Body

The Poodle's neck is *well proportioned, strong and long enough to permit the head to be carried high and with dignity, skin snug at throat. The neck rises from strong, smoothly muscled shoulders. Major fault: ewe neck.*

The topline is *level, neither sloping nor roached, from the highest point of the shoulder blade to the base of the tail, with the exception of a slight hollow just behind the shoulder.*

The Poodle's body *includes a chest deep and moderately wide with well sprung ribs. The loin is short, broad*

*A café-au-lait
Miniature
Poodle.*

*well bent: femur and tibia are about
equal in length; hock to heel short and
perpendicular to the ground. When
standing, the rear toes are only slightly
behind the point of the rump. Major
fault: cow hocks.*

Coat

The Poodle's coat is spectacular, especially when coiffed for show. The
breed standard calls for a coat quality that is *(1) Curly: of naturally harsh
texture, dense throughout. (2) Corded:
hanging in tight even cords of varying
length; longer on mane or body coat,*
*head and ears; shorter on puffs, bracelets,
and pompoms.*

Color

Not only do Poodles come in three
sizes, but they can be found in a
rainbow of coat colors. According
to the breed standard, *the coat is an
even and solid color at the skin. In
blues, grays, silvers, browns, café-au-
laits, apricots and creams the coat
may show varying shades of the same
color. This is frequently present in the
somewhat darker feathering of the ears
and in the tipping of the ruff. While*

THE AMERICAN KENNEL CLUB

Familiarly referred to as "the AKC," the American Kennel Club is a nonprofit organization devoted to the advancement of purebred dogs. The AKC maintains a registry of recognized breeds and adopts and enforces rules for dog events including shows, obedience trials, field trials, hunting tests, lure coursing, herding, earthdog trials, agility and the Canine Good Citizen program. It is a club of clubs, established in 1884 and composed, today, of over 500 autonomous dog clubs throughout the United States. Each club is represented by a delegate; the delegates make up the legislative body of the AKC, voting on rules and electing directors. The American Kennel Club maintains the Stud Book, the record of every dog ever registered with the AKC, and publishes a variety of materials on purebred dogs, including a monthly magazine, books and numerous educational pamphlets. For more information, contact the AKC at the address listed in Chapter 9, "Resources."

clear colors are definitely preferred, such natural variation in the shading of the coat is not to be considered a fault.

Brown and café-au-lait Poodles have liver-colored noses, eye-rims and lips, dark toenails and dark amber eyes. Black, blue, gray, silver, cream and white Poodles have black noses, eye-rims and lips, black or self-colored toenails and very dark eyes. In the apricots, while the foregoing coloring is preferred, liver-colored noses, eye-rims and lips, and amber eyes are permitted.

Generally, black and white are the most common colors; locating a brown, apricot or silver Poodle can be more difficult.

Additionally, most Poodles are not the same color at birth as they are at maturity. In some cases, it takes more than a year for the color to "clear." Silver Poodles, for example, are usually born black and later fade to silver.

Gait

How should a Poodle move? According to the breed standard, a Poodle's *gait is a straightforward trot with light springy action and strong hind-quarters drive. Head and tail carried up. Sound, effortless movement is essential.*

Temperament

The breed standard defines temperament as: *Carrying herself proudly, very active, intelligent, the Poodle has about herself an air of distinction and dignity peculiar to herself. Major fault: shyness or sharpness.*

A brown Miniature Poodle.

Disqualifications

According to the breed standard, Poodles may be disqualified for the following reasons:

SIZE—A dog over or under the specified height limits shall be disqualified.

CLIP—A dog in any type of clip other than those listed under "Coat" shall be disqualified.

PARTI-COLORS—The coat of a parti-colored dog is not an even solid color at the skin but of two or more colors. Parti-colored dogs shall be disqualified.

A silver Miniature Poodle.

What about Poodles who fail to meet the standard set forth by the Poodle Club of America? Certainly, such dogs would not go far in the show ring and should not be bred and allowed to reproduce— at least not by a responsible breeder. Such dogs would be considered as pets, companion animals not to be bred. They are usually spayed or neutered, or shown in obedience.

CHAPTER SEVEN

A Matter of Fact

Poodles have been charming humans for generations. Images of Poodle-like dogs have been found carved on Roman tombs, suggesting that the breed is one of the oldest around today. There are many references to the Poodle in fifteenth- and sixteenth-century art and literature, and the Poodle is said to have been a favorite pet during the eighteenth century—and of King Louis XVI of France. Poodles have been known equally as entertainers: They were performers in Queen Anne's court in England, and they have been circus stars.

Indeed, Poodles enjoy a long history, but tracing their origin is another matter. Much of what is known about yesteryear's Poodle is found in references in literature and art, so mapping a precise history is difficult at best.

FROM WHENCE THEY CAME

Today's Poodle probably originated as a water retriever, and some speculate the breed could be the original Water Spaniel. In sixteenth-century Europe, a dog called the Water Dog of England was quite popular among hunters. It was well suited

The Poodle's curly coat is water repellent, which aids the breed in aquatic duties.

Water Dog; others believe the breeds merged. It is also believed that the Irish Water Spaniel descends from this same lineage. However, some theorize that the Irish Water Spaniel—which sports a curly coat similar to the Poodle and is an adept retriever—is the forerunner of the Poodle.

The Poodle is believed to have originated in Germany, though to name a specific country of origin is impossible. It is probably more accurate to state that the Poodle is a product of the entire European continent. Practically every European country has claimed the Poodle as its own, with Germany, Russia and France being the chief contenders.

It is interesting to note that Spain might be in a better position

for aquatic duties with its strong build, water-repellent coat and webbed feet. Some say today's Poodle is a direct descendant of the

The name Poodle is derived from pudelin— *German for "splashing in water."*

than most European countries to claim origination of the Poodle. This idea is based on the premise that the Poodle is part of the spaniel family, and the word *spaniel* is derived from the word *Spain*. This is where the spaniel developed, even if it did not originate there.

German writings from the sixteenth century describe the Pudel—a word that is derived from the verb *pudelin,* meaning "splashing in water" —as a fairly large, black, water retriever. In the 1600s, in some instances, this Water Dog began to be called a Pudel.

The dog was also found in Belgium and Holland as a working dog called Poedel. Most likely, the English name, Poodle, descends from these terms.

It also seems to have gained national recognition, although there doesn't seem to be irrefutable evidence to prove this idea. French literary references note a "vigorous, intelligent, sturdy, curly-haired dog that goes into the water," a description that matches the English Water Dog and the German Pudel. Most likely, the name "French Poodle" can be attributed to its popularity in France.

The standard-size Poodle is believed to be the oldest among today's three sizes—Toy, Miniature and Standard. The larger Poodles were initially most common, but as Poodle fanciers grew interested in breeding for size, Miniatures and Toys appeared on the scene.

Another more widely accepted theory is that Miniatures are the

Très Français

The French, however, have long claimed the Poodle as their own, hence the common name, "French Poodle." Indeed, the dogs found a devoted following in France. First known as the Barbet (a term that means "beard" and is used to describe any dog with long hair), and later as the Caniche (duck dog), the Poodle was a popular hunting dog.

Poodles are known for being great entertainers.

WHERE DID DOGS COME FROM?

It can be argued that dogs were right there at man's side from the beginning of time. As soon as human beings began to document their existence, the dog was among their drawings and inscriptions. Dogs were not just friends, they served a purpose: There were dogs to hunt birds, pull sleds, herd sheep, burrow after rats—even sit in laps! What your dog was originally bred to do influences the way he behaves. The American Kennel Club recognizes over 140 breeds, and there are hundreds more distinct breeds around the world. To make sense of the breeds, they are grouped according to their size or function. The AKC has seven groups:

1. Sporting
2. Working
3. Herding
4. Hounds
5. Terriers
6. Toys
7. Non Sporting

Can you name a breed from each group? Here's some help: (1) Golden Retriever; (2) Doberman Pinscher; (3) Collie; (4) Beagle; (5) Scottish Terrier; (6) Maltese; and (7) Dalmatian. All modern domestic dogs (*Canis familiaris*) are related, however different they look, and are all descended from *Canis lupus,* the gray wolf.

result of breeding small Standards. Likewise, the Toy is said to be the result of breeding small Miniatures.

CIRCUS DOGS

The Poodle's reputation as a performer or circus animal can be traced to France. As early as 1700, the French discovered the natural, clownish talent of the breed. A troupe of Poodles from France, called "Performing Dogs" or "Dancers," is said to have performed in London for King George III. The dogs pushed a wheelbarrow, danced, jumped through hoops, skipped rope, operated a spinning wheel and tumbled.

Unfortunately, the Poodle was losing its reputation as a hardworking, intelligent, hardy hunting companion and instead was earning a reputation for being a trick dog or high-society pet.

A History of Hair

The elaborate coat styles of the Poodle undoubtedly enhanced the circuslike perception of the breed, but such styling can be traced to the early days of the breed. Early dogs had heavy, water-repellent coats that helped keep them warm while dashing in and out of water. Those dense coats often hampered the dog's movement once wet. The solution was to trim the hair short on the hindquarters, leaving it full around the dog's chest for warmth. Later, "bobbles" were left on to protect the joints from rheumatism. The hair was also tied back from the eyes, first with a string and later with colored ribbon to make the dog more easily visible when swimming or in the field.

Another phenomenon at the time, and one that was considered quite fashionable, was the Corded Poodle. A Corded Poodle is one whose coat is rolled and twisted into long, tight ringlets. Each ropelike ringlet is formed individually, with the help of wax or petroleum jelly, and is left to grow until it reaches the ground. The cords were often tied up in linen to protect them. The Corded Poodle must have been quite a sight, but its popularity waned, probably due to the impracticality of keeping such a coat in condition.

THE POODLE IN THE U.S.

The Poodle was introduced to the United States in the late 1800s, and the first Poodle was registered in the

This white Standard wears the continental cut, which was developed to provide unrestricted movement of the hindquarters and warmth for the chest region.

American Kennel Club Stud Book in 1887. It was not until a group of dedicated fanciers founded the Poodle

FAMOUS OWNERS OF POODLES

Judy Garland

Tipper Gore

Helen Hayes

Carolina Herrera

Sophia Loren

Edgar Allan Poe

Sugar Ray Robinson

Gertrude Stein

John Steinbeck

Tracey Ullman

Club of America in 1931, however, that the breed was generally noticed.

Early Poodles in the United States were imported, for the most part, from England. They were mostly black, white or brown, and the Standard size attracted the most interest. Poodle registration with the American Kennel Club was minimal and few were exhibited at shows.

Both Standard and Toy Poodles were shown before the beginning of World War I, but they were considered separate breeds. As Miniatures became popular, they were shown with the Standards. In competition, however, they were divided into two coat types: curly and corded. The early Toys were considered a separate breed until 1943, when the American Kennel Club recognized them as the third variety of Poodle.

A few enthusiasts, most in the Northeast, worked toward wider acceptance and understanding of the breed, which was considered an object of curiosity rather than an intelligent, talented breed of dog. The newly established breed club set forth a breed standard by which American breeders defined the dog, based on the standard and rules of The Curley Poodle Club of England.

These dedicated efforts on behalf of the Poodle paid off. In 1930, there were only thirty-four Poodles registered with the American Kennel Club; by 1960, there were more Poodles registered with the American Kennel Club than any other breed. In 1997, the Poodle was the AKC's fifth most popular breed with 54,774 Poodles registered.

Today's Poodle

The Poodle we know today comes in three sizes and myriad coat colors, and it is intelligent and a wonderful companion. But most of all, the Poodle's ancestry and history show the breed's versatility. From hunting companion, to circus entertainer, to family pet and show dog, the Poodle has the ability—and talent—to adapt to a variety of circumstances.

Is the Poodle still hunting? Yes, and those who work their dogs in the field swear by their retrieving talents. The Poodle is a great showman and often brings home blue ribbons from a dog show. The Poodle does not just have good looks; it also performs well in obedience trials.

Most important, the Poodle today is a popular, devoted companion to all who own him.

CHAPTER EIGHT

On Good Behavior

by Ian Dunbar, Ph.D., MRCVS

Training is the jewel in the crown—the most important aspect of doggy husbandry. There is no more important variable influencing dog behavior and temperament than the dog's education: A well-trained, well-behaved and good-natured puppydog is always a joy to live with, but an untrained and uncivilized dog can be a perpetual nightmare. Moreover, deny the dog an education and she will not have the opportunity to fulfill her own canine potential; neither will she have the ability to communicate effectively with her human companions.

Luckily, modern psychological training methods are easy, efficient, effective and, above all, considerably dog-friendly and user-friendly. Doggy education is as simple as it is enjoyable. But before you can have a good time play-training with your new dog, you have to learn what to do and how to do it. There is no bigger variable influencing the success of dog training than the owner's experience and expertise. Before you embark on the dog's education, you must first educate yourself.

BASIC TRAINING FOR OWNERS

Ideally, basic owner training should begin well before you select your dog. Find out all you can about your chosen breed first, then master rudimentary training and handling skills. If you already have your puppydog, owner training is a dire emergency—the clock is ticking! Especially for puppies, the first few weeks at home are the most important and influential days in the dog's life. Indeed, the cause of most adolescent and adult problems may be traced back to the initial days the pup explores her new home. This is the time to establish the *status quo*—to teach the puppydog how you would like her to be-

Knowing what to expect of your puppy prior to her arrival in your home is a great way to stop behavior problems before they start.

have and so prevent otherwise quite predictable problems.

In addition to consulting breeders and breed books such as this one (which understandably have a positive breed bias), seek out as many pet owners with your breed as you can find. Good points are obvious. What you want to find out are the breed-specific problems, so you can nip them in the bud. In particular, you should talk to owners with adolescent dogs and make a list of all anticipated problems. Most important, test drive at least half a dozen adolescent and adult dogs of your breed yourself. An 8-week-old puppy is deceptively easy to handle, but she will acquire adult size, speed and strength in just four months, so you should learn now what to prepare for.

Puppy and pet dog training classes offer a convenient venue to locate pet owners and observe dogs in action. For a list of suitable trainers in your area, contact the Association of Pet Dog Trainers (see chapter 9). You may also begin your basic owner training by observing other owners in class. Watch as many classes and test drive as many dogs as possible. Select an upbeat, dog-friendly, people-friendly, fun-and-games, puppydog pet training class to learn the ropes. Also, watch training videos and read training books. You must find out what to do and how to do it *before* you have to do it.

PRINCIPLES OF TRAINING

Most people think training comprises teaching the dog to do things such as sit, speak and roll over, but even a 4-week-old pup knows how to do these things already. Instead, the first step in training involves teaching the dog human words for each dog behavior and activity and for each aspect of the dog's environment. That way you, the owner, can more easily participate in the dog's domestic education by directing her to perform specific actions appropriately, that is, at the right time, in the right place and so on. Training opens communication channels, enabling an educated dog to at least understand her owner's requests.

In addition to teaching a dog what we want her to do, it is also necessary to teach her why she should do what we ask. Indeed, 95 percent of training revolves around motivating the dog to want to do what we want. Dogs often understand what

their owners want; they just don't see the point of doing it—especially when the owner's repetitively boring and seemingly senseless instructions are totally at odds with much more pressing and exciting doggy distractions. It is not so much the dog that is being stubborn or dominant; rather, it is the owner who has failed to acknowledge the dog's needs and feelings and to approach training from the dog's point of view.

The Meaning of Instructions

The secret to successful training is learning how to use training lures to predict or prompt specific behaviors—to coax the dog to do what you want when you want. Any highly valued object (such as a treat or toy) may be used as a lure, which the dog will follow with her eyes and nose. Moving the lure in specific ways entices the dog to move her nose, head and entire body in specific ways. In fact, by learning the art of manipulating various lures, it is possible to teach the dog to assume virtually any body position and perform any action. Once you have control over the expression of the dog's behaviors and can elicit any

63

You can quickly train your dog to do virtually anything when using the lure-reward method, and it is enjoyable for dogs, too!

body position or behavior at will, you can easily teach the dog to perform on request.

Tell your dog what you want her to do, use a lure to entice her to respond correctly, then profusely praise and maybe reward her once she performs the desired action. For example, verbally request "Fido, sit!" while you move a squeaky toy upwards and backwards over the dog's muzzle (lure-movement and hand signal), smile knowingly as she looks up (to follow the lure) and sits down (as a result of canine anatomical engineering), then praise her to distraction ("Gooood Fido!"). Squeak the toy, offer a training treat and

give your dog and yourself a pat on the back.

Being able to elicit desired responses over and over enables the owner to reward the dog over and over. Consequently, the dog begins to think training is fun. For example, the more the dog is rewarded for sitting, the more she enjoys sitting. Eventually the dog comes to realize that, whereas most sitting is appreciated, sitting immediately upon request usually prompts especially enthusiastic praise and a slew of high-level rewards. The dog begins to sit on cue much of the time, showing that she is starting to grasp the meaning of the owner's verbal request and hand signal.

Why Comply?

Most dogs enjoy initial lure-reward training and are only too happy to comply with their owners' wishes. Unfortunately, repetitive drilling without appreciative feedback tends to diminish the dog's enthusiasm until she eventually fails to see the point of complying anymore. Moreover, as the dog approaches adolescence she becomes more easily distracted as she develops other interests. Lengthy sessions with repetitive exercises tend to bore and demotivate both parties. If it's not fun, the owner doesn't do it and neither does the dog.

Integrate training into your dog's life: The greater number of training sessions each day and the shorter they are, the more willingly compliant your dog will become. Make sure to have a short (just a few seconds) training interlude before every enjoyable canine activity. For example, ask your dog to sit to greet people, to sit before you throw her Frisbee and to sit for her supper. Really, sitting is no different from a canine "Please." Also, include numerous short training interludes during every enjoyable canine pastime, for example, when playing with the dog or when she is running in the park. In this fashion, doggy distractions may be effectively converted into rewards for training. Just as all games have rules, fun becomes training . . . and training becomes fun.

Eventually, rewards actually become unnecessary to continue motivating your dog. If trained with consideration and kindness, performing the desired behaviors will become self-rewarding and, in a sense, your dog will motivate herself. Just as it is not necessary to reward a human companion during an enjoyable

OWNING A PARTY ANIMAL

It's a fact: The more of the world your puppy is exposed to, the more comfortable she'll be in it. Once your puppy's had her shots, start taking her everywhere with you. Encourage friendly interaction with strangers, expose her to different environments (towns, fields, beaches), and most important, enroll her in a puppy class where she'll get to play with other puppies. These simple, fun, shared activities will develop your pup into a confident extrovert, reliable around other people and other dogs.

walk in the park, or following a game of tennis, it is hardly necessary to reward our best friend—the dog— for walking by our side or while playing fetch. Human company during enjoyable activities is reward enough for most dogs.

Even though your dog has become self-motivating, it's still good to praise and pet her a lot and offer rewards once in a while, especially for a job well done. And if for no other reason, praising and rewarding others is good for the human heart.

Punishment

Without a doubt, lure-reward training is by far the best way to teach:

65

Punishment training does not stop your pet from misbehaving. Instead, it teaches your pet to perform the action when (or where) you can't see it.

Entice your dog to do what you want and then reward her for doing so. Unfortunately, a human shortcoming is to take the good for granted and to moan and groan at the bad. Specifically, the dog's many good behaviors are ignored while the owner focuses on punishing the dog for making mistakes. In extreme cases, instruction is limited to punishing mistakes made by a trainee dog, child, employee or husband, even though it has been proven punishment training is notoriously inefficient and ineffective and is decidedly unfriendly and combative. It teaches the dog that training is a drag, almost as quickly as it teaches the dog to dislike her trainer. Why treat our best friends like our worst enemies?

Punishment training is also much more laborious and time-consuming. Whereas it takes only a finite amount of time to teach a dog what to chew, for example, it takes much, much longer to punish the dog for each and every mistake. Remember, there is only one right way! So why not teach that right way from the outset?!

To make matters worse, punishment training causes severe lapses in the dog's reliability. Since it is obviously impossible to punish the dog each and every time she misbehaves, the dog quickly learns to distinguish between those times when she must comply (so as to avoid impending punishment) and those times when she need not comply because punishment is impossible. Such times include when the dog is off leash and 6 feet away when the owner is otherwise engaged (talking to a friend, watching television, taking a shower, tending to the baby or chatting on the telephone) or when the dog is left at home alone.

Instances of misbehavior will be numerous when the owner is away because even when the dog complied in the owner's looming presence, she did so unwillingly. The dog was forced to act against her will, rather than molding her will to want to please. Hence, when the owner is absent, not only does the dog know she need not comply, she simply does not want to. Again, the trainee is not a stubborn vindictive beast, but rather the trainer has failed to teach. Punishment training invariably creates unpredictable Jekyll and Hyde behavior.

TRAINER'S TOOLS

Many training books extol the virtues of a vast array of training paraphernalia and electronic and metallic gizmos, most of which are designed for canine restraint, correction and punishment, rather than for actual facilitation of doggy education. In reality, most effective training tools are not found in stores; they come from within ourselves. In addition to a willing dog, all you really need is a functional human brain, gentle hands, a loving heart and a good attitude.

In terms of equipment, all dogs do require a quality buckle collar to sport dog tags and to attach the leash (for safety and to comply with local leash laws). Hollow chew toys (like Kongs or sterilized longbones) and a dog bed or collapsible crate are musts for housetraining. Three additional tools are required:

1. specific lures (training treats and toys) to predict and prompt specific desired behaviors;

2. rewards (praise, affection, training treats and toys) to reinforce

for the dog what a lot of fun it all is; and

3. knowledge—how to convert the dog's favorite activities and games (potential distractions to training) into "life-rewards," which may be employed to facilitate training.

The most powerful of these is knowledge. Education is the key! Watch training classes, participate in training classes, watch videos, read books, enjoy play-training with your dog and then your dog will say "Please," and your dog will say "Thank you!"

HOUSETRAINING

If dogs were left to their own devices, certainly they would chew, dig and bark for entertainment and then no doubt highlight a few areas of their living space with sprinkles of urine, in much the same way we decorate by hanging pictures. Consequently, when we ask a dog to live with us, we must teach her *where* she may dig, *where* she may perform her toilet duties, *what* she may chew and *when* she may bark. After all, when left at home alone for many hours, we cannot expect the dog to amuse herself by completing crosswords or watching TV!

Also, it would be decidedly unfair to keep the house rules a secret from the dog, and then get angry and punish the poor critter for inevitably transgressing rules she did not even know existed. Remember: Without adequate education and guidance, the dog will be forced to establish her own rules—doggy rules—and most probably will be at odds with the owner's view of domestic living.

Since most problems develop during the first few days the dog is at home, prospective dog owners must be certain they are quite clear about the principles of housetraining *before* they get a dog. Early misbehaviors quickly become established as the *status quo*—becoming firmly entrenched as hard-to-break bad habits, which set the precedent for years to come. Make sure to teach your dog good habits right from the start. Good habits are just as hard to break as bad ones!

Ideally, when a new dog comes home, try to arrange for someone to be present as much as possible during the first few days (for adult dogs) or weeks for puppies. With only a little forethought, it is surprisingly easy to find a puppy sitter, such as a retired person, who would be willing to eat from your refrigerator and watch your television while keeping an eye on the newcomer to encourage the dog to play with chew toys and to ensure she goes outside on a regular basis.

Potty Training

Follow these steps to teach the dog where she should relieve herself:

1. never let her make a single mistake;

2. let her know where you want her to go; and

3. handsomely reward her for doing so: "GOOOOOOOD DOG!!!" liver treat, liver treat, liver treat!

Preventing Mistakes

A single mistake is a training disaster, since it heralds many more in future weeks. And each time the dog soils the house, this further reinforces the dog's unfortunate preference for an indoor, carpeted toilet. Do not let an unhousetrained dog have full run of the house.

When you are away from home, or cannot pay full attention, confine

HOUSETRAINING 1-2-3

1. Prevent Mistakes. When you can't supervise your puppy, confine her in a single room or in her crate (but don't leave her for too long!). Puppy-proof the area by laying down newspapers so that if she does make a mistake it won't matter.

2. Teach Where. Take your puppy to the spot you want her to use every hour.

3. When she goes, praise her profusely and give her three favorite treats.

69

the dog to an area where elimination is appropriate, such as an outdoor run or, better still, a small, comfortable indoor kennel with access to an outdoor run. When confined in this manner, most dogs will naturally housetrain themselves.

If that's not possible, confine the dog to an area, such as a utility room, kitchen, basement or garage, where elimination may not be desired in the long run but as an interim measure it is certainly preferable to doing it all around the house. Use newspaper to cover the floor of the dog's day room. The newspaper may be used to soak up the urine and to wrap up and dispose of the feces. Once your dog develops a preferred spot for eliminating, it is only necessary to cover that part of the floor with newspaper. The smaller papered area may then be moved (only a little each day) towards the door to the outside. Thus the dog will develop the tendency to go to the door when she needs to relieve herself.

Never confine an unhousetrained dog to a crate for long periods. Doing so would force the dog to soil the crate and ruin its usefulness as an aid for housetraining (see the following discussion).

Teaching Where

In order to teach your dog where you would like her to do her business, you have to be there to direct the proceedings—an obvious, yet often neglected, fact of life. In order to be there to teach the dog where to go, you need to know *when* she needs to go. Indeed, the success of housetraining depends on the owner's ability to predict these times. Certainly, a regular feeding schedule will facilitate prediction somewhat, but there is nothing like "loading the deck" and influencing the timing of the outcome yourself!

Whenever you are at home, make sure the dog is under constant supervision and/or confined to a small area. If already well trained, simply instruct the dog to lie down in her bed or basket. Alternatively, confine the dog to a crate (doggy den) or tie-down (a short, 18-inch lead that can be clipped to an eye hook in the baseboard near her bed). Short-term close confinement strongly inhibits urination and defecation, since the dog does not want to soil her sleeping area. Thus, when you release the puppydog each hour, she will definitely need to urinate immediately and defecate every third or fourth hour. Keep the dog confined to her doggy den and take her to her intended toilet area each hour, every hour on the hour. When taking your dog outside, instruct her to sit quietly before opening the door—she will soon learn to sit by the door when she needs to go out!

Teaching Why

Being able to predict when the dog needs to go enables the owner to be on the spot to praise and reward the dog. Each hour, hurry the dog to the intended toilet area in the yard, issue the appropriate instruction ("Go pee!"

or "Go poop!"), then give the dog
three to four minutes to produce.
Praise and offer a couple of training
treats when successful. The treats are
important because many people fail
to praise their dogs with feeling . . .
and housetraining is hardly the
time for understatement. So either
loosen up and enthusiastically praise
that dog: "Wuzzzer-wuzzer-wuzzer,
hoooser good wuffer den? Hoooo
went pee for Daddy?" Or say "Good
dog!" as best you can and offer the
treats for effect.

Following elimination is an ideal
time for a spot of play-training in the
yard or house. Also, an empty dog
may be allowed greater freedom
around the house for the next half
hour or so, just as long as you keep
an eye out to make sure she does not
get into other kinds of mischief. If
you are preoccupied and cannot pay
full attention, confine the dog to
her doggy den once more to enjoy a
peaceful snooze or to play with her
many chew toys.

If your dog does not eliminate
within the allotted time outside—
no biggie! Back to her doggy den,
and then try again after another
hour.

As I own large dogs, I always
feel more relaxed walking an empty

dog, knowing that I will not need to
finish our stroll weighted down with
bags of feces!

Beware of falling into the trap of
walking the dog to get her to eliminate. The good ol' dog walk is such
an enormous highlight in the dog's
life that it represents the single biggest potential reward in domestic
dogdom. However, when in a hurry,
or during inclement weather, many
owners abruptly terminate the walk
the moment the dog has done her
business. This, in effect, severely
punishes the dog for doing the right
thing, in the right place, at the right
time. Consequently, many dogs
become strongly inhibited from eliminating outdoors because they know
it will signal an abrupt end to an
otherwise thoroughly enjoyable walk.

Instead, instruct the dog to relieve herself in the yard prior to going for a walk. If you follow the
above instructions, most dogs soon
learn to eliminate on cue. As soon
as the dog eliminates, praise (and
offer a treat or two)—"Good dog!
Let's go walkies!" Use the walk as
a reward for eliminating in the yard.
If the dog does not go, put her back
in her doggy den and think about
a walk later on. You will find with
a "No feces—no walk" policy, your

71

Introducing your puppy to the chew toy will keep her from chewing up your shoes, and chew toys will certainly remain your pet's favorite hobby into her adult years.

72

dog will become one of the fastest defecators in the business.

If you do not have a backyard, instruct the dog to eliminate right outside your front door prior to the walk. Not only will this facilitate cleanup and disposal of the feces in your own trash can but, also, the walk may again be used as a colossal reward.

CHEWING AND BARKING

Short-term close confinement also teaches the dog that occasional quiet moments are a reality of domestic living. Your puppydog is extremely impressionable during her first few weeks at home. Regular confinement at this time soon exerts a calming

influence over the dog's personality. Remember, once the dog is house-trained and calmer, there will be a whole lifetime ahead for the dog to enjoy full run of the house and garden. On the other hand, by letting the newcomer have unrestricted access to the entire household and allowing her to run willy-nilly, she will most certainly develop a bunch of behavior problems in short order, no doubt necessitating confinement later in life. It would not be fair to remedially restrain and confine a dog you have trained, through neglect, to run free.

When confining the dog, make sure she always has an impressive array of suitable chew toys. Kongs and sterilized longbones (both readily available from pet stores) make the best chew toys, since they are hollow and may be stuffed with treats to heighten the dog's interest. For example, by stuffing the little hole at the top of a Kong with a small piece of freeze-dried liver, the dog will not want to leave it alone.

Remember, treats do not have to be junk food and they certainly should not represent extra calories. Rather, treats should be part of each dog's regular daily diet: Some food may be served in the dog's bowl for breakfast and dinner, some food may be used as training treats and some food may be used for stuffing chew toys. I regularly stuff my dogs' many Kongs with different shaped biscuits and kibble. The kibble seems to fall out fairly easily, as do the oval-shaped biscuits, thus rewarding the dog instantaneously for checking out the chew toys. The bone-shaped biscuits fall out after a while, rewarding the dog for worrying at the chew toy. But the triangular biscuits never come out. They remain inside the Kong as lures, maintaining the dog's fascination with her chew toy. To further focus the dog's interest, I always make sure to flavor the triangular biscuits by rubbing them with a little cheese or freeze-dried liver.

If stuffed chew toys are reserved especially for times the dog is confined, the puppydog will soon learn to enjoy quiet moments in her doggy den and she will quickly develop a chew-toy habit—a good habit! This is a simple autoshaping process; all the owner has to do is set up the situation and the dog all but trains herself—easy and effective. Even when the dog is given run of the house, her first inclination will be to indulge her rewarding chew-toy habit rather than destroy less-attractive household articles, such as curtains, carpets, chairs and compact disks. Similarly, a chew-toy chewer will be less inclined to scratch and chew herself excessively. Also, if the dog busies herself as a recreational chewer, she will be less inclined to develop into a recreational barker or digger when left at home alone.

Stuff a number of chew toys whenever the dog is left confined and remove the extra-special-tasting treats when you return. Your dog will now amuse herself with her chew toys before falling asleep and then resume playing with her chew toys when she expects you to return. Since most owner-absent misbehavior happens

TOYS THAT EARN THEIR KEEP

To entertain even the most distracted of dogs, while you're home or away, have a selection of the following toys on hand: hollow chew toys (like Kongs, sterilized hollow longbones and cubes or balls that can be stuffed with kibble). Smear peanut butter or cheese spread on the inside of the hollow toy or bone and stuff the bone with kibble and your dog will think of nothing else but working the object to get at the food. Great to take your dog's mind off the fact that you've left the house.

*To teach come,
call your dog,
open your arms
as a welcoming
signal, wave a
toy or a treat
and praise for
every step in
your direction.*

74

right after you leave and right before your expected return, your puppydog will now be conveniently preoccupied with her chew toys at these times.

COME AND SIT

Most puppies will happily approach virtually anyone, whether called or not; that is, until they collide with adolescence and develop other more important doggy interests, such as sniffing a multiplicity of exquisite odors on the grass. Your mission, Mr./Ms. Owner, is to teach and reward the pup for coming reliably, willingly and happily when called—and you have just three months to get it done. Unless adequately reinforced, your puppy's tendency to approach people will self-destruct by adolescence.

Call your dog ("Fido, come!"), open your arms (and maybe squat down) as a welcoming signal, waggle a treat or toy as a lure and reward the puppydog when she comes running. Do not wait to praise the dog until she reaches you—she may come 95 percent of the way and then run off after some distraction. Instead, praise the dog's first step towards you and continue praising enthusiastically for every step she takes in your direction.

When the rapidly approaching puppydog is three lengths away from impact, instruct her to sit ("Fido, sit!") and hold the lure in front of you in an outstretched hand to prevent her from hitting you mid-chest and knocking you flat on your back! As Fido decelerates to nose the lure, move the treat upwards and backwards just over her muzzle with an upwards motion of your extended arm (palm-upwards). As the dog looks up to follow the lure, she will sit down (if she jumps up, you are holding the lure too high). Praise the dog for sitting. Move backwards and call her again. Repeat this many times over, always praising when Fido comes and sits; on occasion, reward her.

For the first couple of trials, use a training treat both as a lure to entice the dog to come and sit and as a reward for doing so. Thereafter, try to use different items as lures and rewards. For example, lure the dog with a Kong or Frisbee but reward her with a food treat. Or lure the dog with a food treat but pat her and throw a tennis ball as a reward. After just a few repetitions, dispense with the lures and rewards; the dog will begin to respond willingly to your verbal requests and hand signals just for the prospect of praise from your heart and affection from your hands.

Instruct every family member, friend and visitor how to get the dog to come and sit. Invite people over for a series of pooch parties; do not keep the pup a secret—let other people enjoy this puppy, and let the pup enjoy other people. Puppydog parties are not only fun, they easily attract a lot of people to help you train your dog. Unless you teach your dog how to meet people, that is, to sit for greetings, no doubt the dog will resort to jumping up. Then you and the visitors will get annoyed, and the dog will be punished. This is not fair. Send out those invitations for puppy parties and teach your dog to be mannerly and socially acceptable.

Even though your dog quickly masters obedient recalls in the house, her reliability may falter when playing in the backyard or local park. Ironically, it is the owner who has unintentionally trained the dog not to respond in these instances. By allowing the dog to play and run around and otherwise have a good time, but then to call the dog to put her on leash to take her home, the dog quickly learns playing is fun but training is a drag. Thus, playing in the park becomes a severe distraction, which works against training. Bad news!

Instead, whether playing with the dog off leash or on leash, request her to come at frequent intervals—say, every minute or so. On most occasions, praise and pet the dog for a few seconds while she is sitting,

Using a food
lure to teach
"Sit," "Down"
and "Stand."
1) "Phoenix, Sit."
2) Hand palm
upwards, move
lure up and
back over dog's
muzzle.
3) "Good sit,
Phoenix!"

4) "Phoenix,
Down."
5) Hand palm
downwards,
move lure down
to lie between
dog's forepaws.
6) "Phoenix,
Off. Good down,
Phoenix!"

7) "Phoenix,
Sit!"
8) Palm
upwards, move
lure up and
back, keeping it
close to dog's
muzzle.
9) "Good sit,
Phoenix!"

10) *"Phoenix, Stand!"*
11) *Move lure away from dog at nose height, then lower it a tad.*
12) *"Phoenix, Off! Good stand, Phoenix!"*

13) *"Phoenix, Down!"*
14) *Hand palm downwards, move lure down to lie between dog's forepaws.*
15) *"Phoenix, Off! Good down-stay, Phoenix!"*

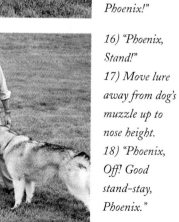

16) *"Phoenix, Stand!"*
17) *Move lure away from dog's muzzle up to nose height.*
18) *"Phoenix, Off! Good stand-stay, Phoenix."*

then tell her to go play again. For especially fast recalls, offer a couple of training treats and take the time to praise and pet the dog enthusiastically before releasing her. The dog will learn that coming when called is not necessarily the end of the play session, and neither is it the end of the world; rather, it signals an enjoyable, quality time-out with the owner before resuming play once more. In fact, playing in the park now becomes a very effective life-reward, which works to facilitate training by reinforcing each obedient and timely recall. Good news!

SIT, DOWN, STAND AND ROLLOVER

Teaching the dog a variety of body positions is easy for owner and dog, impressive for spectators and extremely useful for all. Using lure-reward techniques, it is possible to train several positions at once to verbal commands or hand signals (which impress the socks off onlookers).

Sit and down—the two control commands—prevent or resolve nearly a hundred behavior problems. For example, if the dog happily and obediently sits or lies down when requested, she cannot jump on visitors, dash out the front door, run around and chase her tail, pester other dogs, harass cats or annoy family, friends or strangers. Additionally, "Sit" or "Down" are the best emergency commands for off-leash control.

It is easier to teach and maintain a reliable sit than maintain a reliable recall. Sit is the purest and simplest of commands—either the dog is sitting or she is not. If there is any change of circumstances or potential danger in the park, for example, simply instruct the dog to sit. If she sits, you have a number of options: Allow the dog to resume playing when she is safe, walk up and put the dog on leash or call the dog. The dog will be much more likely to come when called if she has already acknowledged her compliance by sitting. If the dog does not sit in the park—train her to!

Stand and rollover-stay are the two positions for examining the dog. Your veterinarian will love you to distraction if you take a little time to teach the dog to stand still and roll over and play possum. Also, your vet bills will be smaller because it will take the veterinarian less time to examine your dog. The roll-over-stay is an especially useful command

and is really just a variation of the down-stay: Whereas the dog lies prone in the traditional down, she lies supine in the roll-over-stay.

As with teaching come and sit, the training techniques to teach the dog to assume all other body positions on cue are user-friendly and dog-friendly. Simply give the appropriate request, lure the dog into the desired body position using a training treat or toy and then praise (and maybe reward) the dog as soon as she complies. Try not to touch the dog to get her to respond. If you teach the dog by guiding her into position, the dog will quickly learn that rump-pressure means sit, for example, but as yet you still have no control over your dog if she is just 6 feet away. It will still be necessary to teach the dog to sit on request. So do not make training a time-consuming two-step process; instead, teach the dog to sit to a verbal request or hand signal from the outset. Once the dog sits willingly when requested, by all means use your hands to pet the dog when she does so.

To teach down when the dog is already sitting, say "Fido, down!", hold the lure in one hand (palm down) and lower that hand to the floor between the dog's forepaws. As the dog

lowers her head to follow the lure, slowly move the lure away from the dog just a fraction (in front of her paws). The dog will lie down as she stretches her nose forward to follow the lure. Praise the dog when she does so. If the dog stands up, you pulled the lure away too far and too quickly.

When teaching the dog to lie down from the standing position, say "Down" and lower the lure to the floor as before. Once the dog has lowered her forequarters and assumed a play bow, gently and slowly move the lure towards the dog between her forelegs. Praise the dog as soon as her rear end plops down.

After just a couple of trials it will be possible to alternate sits and downs and have the dog energetically perform doggy push-ups. Praise the dog a lot, and after half a dozen or so push-ups reward the dog with a training treat or toy. You will notice the more energetically you move your arm—upwards (palm up) to get the dog to sit, and downwards (palm down) to get the dog to lie down—the more energetically the dog responds to your requests. Now try training the dog in silence and you will notice she has also learned to respond

79

FINDING A TRAINER

Have fun with your dog, take a training class! But don't just sign on any dotted line, find a trainer whose approach and style you like and whose students (and their dogs) are really learning. Ask to visit a class to observe a trainer in action. For the names of trainers near you, ask your veterinarian, your pet supply store, your dog-owning neighbors or call (800) PET-DOGS (the Association of Pet Dog Trainers).

to hand signals. Yeah! Not too shabby for the first session.

To teach stand from the sitting position, say "Fido, stand," slowly move the lure half a dog-length away from the dog's nose, keeping it at nose level, and praise the dog as she stands to follow the lure. As soon as the dog stands, lower the lure to just beneath the dog's chin to entice her to look down; otherwise, she will stand and then sit immediately. To prompt the dog to stand from the down position, move the lure half a dog-length upwards and away from the dog, holding the lure at standing nose height from the floor.

Teaching rollover is best started from the down position, with the dog lying on one side, or at least with both hind legs stretched out on the same side. Say "Fido, bang!" and move the lure backwards and alongside the dog's muzzle to her elbow (on the side of her outstretched hind legs). Once the dog looks to the side and backwards, very slowly move the lure upwards to the dog's shoulder and backbone. Tickling the dog in the goolies (groin area) often invokes a reflex-raising of the hind leg as an appeasement gesture, which facilitates the tendency to roll over. If you move the lure too quickly and the dog jumps into the standing position, have patience and start again. As soon as the dog rolls onto her back, keep the lure stationary and mesmerize the dog with a relaxing tummy rub.

To teach rollover-stay when the dog is standing or moving, say "Fido, bang!" and give the appropriate hand signal (with index finger pointed and thumb cocked in true Sam Spade fashion), then in one fluid movement lure her to first lie down and then rollover-stay as above.

Teaching the dog to stay in each of the above four positions becomes a piece of cake after first teaching the dog not to worry at the toy or treat training lure. This is best accomplished by hand feeding dinner kibble. Hold a piece of kibble firmly in your hand and softly instruct "Off!" Ignore any licking and slobbering for however long the dog worries at the treat, but say "Take it!" and offer the kibble the instant the dog breaks contact with her muzzle. Repeat this a few times, and then up the ante and insist the dog remove her muzzle for one whole second before offering the kibble. Then progressively refine your criteria and have the dog not touch your hand (or treat) for longer and longer periods on each trial, such as for two seconds, four seconds, then six, ten, fifteen, twenty, thirty seconds and so on.

The dog soon learns: (1) worrying at the treat never gets results, whereas (2) noncontact is often rewarded after a variable time lapse.

Teaching "Off!" has many useful applications in its own right. Additionally, instructing the dog not to touch a training lure often produces spontaneous and magical stays. Request the dog to stand-stay, for example, and not to touch the lure. At first set your sights on a short two-second stay before rewarding the dog. (Remember, every long journey begins with a single step.) However, on subsequent trials, gradually and progressively increase the length of stay required to receive a reward.

In no time at all your dog will stand calmly for a minute or so.

RELEVANCY TRAINING

Once you have taught the dog what you expect her to do when requested to come, sit, lie down, stand, roll over and stay, the time is right to teach the dog why she should comply with your wishes. The secret is to have many (many) extremely short training interludes (two to five seconds each) at numerous (numerous) times during the course of the dog's day. Especially work with the dog immediately before the dog's good times and during the dog's good times. For example, ask your dog to sit and/or lie down each time before opening doors, serving meals, offering treats and tummy rubs; ask the dog to perform a few controlled doggy push-ups before letting her off leash or throwing a tennis ball; and perhaps request the dog to sit-down-sit-stand-down-stand-rollover before inviting her to cuddle on the couch.

Similarly, request the dog to sit many times during play or on walks, and in no time at all the dog will be only too pleased to follow your instructions because she has learned that a compliant response heralds all sorts of goodies. Basically all you are trying to teach the dog is how to say please: "Please throw the tennis ball. Please may I snuggle on the couch."

Remember, it is important to keep training interludes short and to have many short sessions each and every day. The shortest (and most useful) session comprises asking the dog to sit and then go play during a play session. When trained this way, your dog will soon associate training with good times. In fact, the dog may be unable to distinguish between training and good times and, indeed, there should be no distinction. The warped concept that training involves forcing the dog to comply and/or dominating her will is totally at odds with the picture of a truly well-trained dog. In reality,

You don't have to walk the dog just for excretory purposes. Teaching your dog to relieve herself before the walk will make the walk more enjoyable for both of you.

enjoying a game of training with a dog is no different from enjoying a game of backgammon or tennis with a friend; and walking with a dog should be no different from strolling with a spouse or with buddies on the golf course.

WALK BY YOUR SIDE

Many people attempt to teach a dog to heel by putting her on a leash and physically correcting the dog when she makes mistakes. There are a number of things seriously wrong with this approach, the first being that most people do not want precision heeling; rather, they simply want the dog to follow or walk by their side. Second, when physically restrained during "training," even though the dog may grudgingly mope by your side when "handcuffed" on leash, let's see what happens when she is off leash. History! The dog is in the next county because she never enjoyed walking with you on leash and you have no control over her off leash. So let's just teach the dog off leash from the outset to want to walk with us. Third, if the dog has not been trained to heel, it is a trifle hasty to think about punishing the poor dog for making mistakes and breaking heeling rules she didn't even know existed. This is simply not fair! Surely, if the dog had been adequately taught how to heel, she would seldom make mistakes and hence there would be no need to correct the dog. Remember, each mistake and each correction (punishment) advertise the trainer's inadequacy, not the dog's. The dog is not stubborn, she is not stupid and she is not bad. Even if she were, she would still require training, so let's train her properly.

Let's teach the dog to enjoy following us and to want to walk by our side off leash. Then it will be easier to teach high-precision off-leash heeling patterns if desired. Before going on outdoor walks, it is necessary to teach the dog not to pull. Then it becomes easy to teach on-leash walking and heeling because the dog already wants to walk with you, she is familiar with the desired walking and heeling positions and she knows not to pull.

FOLLOWING

Start by training your dog to follow you. Many puppies will follow if you simply walk away from them and maybe click your fingers or chuckle. Adult dogs may require additional enticement to stimulate them to follow, such as a training lure or, at the very least, a lively trainer. To teach the dog to follow: (1) keep walking and (2) walk away from the dog. If the dog attempts to lead or lag, change pace; slow down if the dog forges too far ahead, but speed up if she lags too far behind. Say "Steady!" or "Easy!" each time before you slow down and "Quickly!" or "Hustle!" each time before you speed up, and the dog will learn to change pace on

If your dog starts pulling on leash, stand still and wait for her to stop resisting. Be sure not to pull on the leash and to praise her when she finally sits still.

cue. If the dog lags or leads too far, or if she wanders right or left, simply walk quickly in the opposite direction and maybe even run away from the dog and hide.

Practicing is a lot of fun; you can set up a course in your home, yard or park to do this. Indoors, entice the dog to follow upstairs, into a bedroom, into the bathroom, downstairs, around the living room couch, zigzagging between dining room chairs and into the kitchen for dinner. Outdoors, get the dog to follow around park benches, trees, shrubs and along walkways and lines in the grass. (For safety outdoors, it is advisable to attach a long line on the dog, but never exert corrective tension on the line.)

Remember, following has a lot to do with attitude—your attitude! Most probably your dog will not want to follow Mr. Grumpy Troll with the personality of wilted lettuce. Lighten up—walk with a jaunty step, whis-tle a happy tune, sing, skip and tell jokes to your dog, and she will be right there by your side.

BY YOUR SIDE

It is smart to train the dog to walk close on one side or the other—either side will do, your choice. When walking, jogging or cycling, it is generally bad news to have the dog suddenly cut in front of you. In fact, I train my dogs to walk "By my side" and "Other side"—both very useful instructions. It is possible to position the dog fairly accurately by looking to the appropriate side and clicking your fingers or slapping your thigh on that side. A precise positioning may be attained by holding a training lure, such as a chew toy, tennis ball or food treat. Stop and stand still several times throughout the walk, just as you would when window-shopping or meeting a friend. Use the lure to make sure the dog slows down and stays close whenever you stop.

When teaching the dog to heel, we generally want her to sit in heel position when we stop. Teach heel position at the standstill and the dog will learn that the default heel position is sitting by your side (left or right—your choice, unless you wish to compete in obedience trials, in which case the dog must heel on the left).

Several times a day, stand up and call your dog to come and sit in heel position—"Fido, heel!" For example, instruct the dog to come to heel each time there are commercials on

TV, or each time you turn a page of a novel, and the dog will get it in a single evening.

Practice straight-line heeling and turns separately. With the dog sitting at heel, teach her to turn in place. After each quarter-turn, half-turn or full turn in place, lure the dog to sit at heel. Now it's time for short straight-line heeling sequences, no more than a few steps at a time. Always think of heeling in terms of sit-heel-sit sequences—start and end with the dog in position and do your best to keep her there when moving. Progressively increase the number of steps in each sequence. When the dog remains close for 20 yards of straight-line heeling, it is time to add a few turns and then sign up for a happy-heeling obedience class to get some advice from the experts.

NO PULLING ON LEASH

You can start teaching your dog not to pull on leash anywhere—in front of the television or outdoors—but regardless of location, you must not take a single step with tension in the leash. For a reason known only to dogs, even just a couple of paces of pulling on leash is intrinsically moti-

vating and diabolically rewarding. Instead, attach the leash to the dog's collar, grasp the other end firmly with both hands held close to your chest and stand still—do not budge an inch. Have somebody watch you with a stopwatch to time your progress, or else you will never believe this will work; and so you will not even try the exercise, and your shoulder and the dog's neck will be traumatized for years to come.

Stand still and wait for the dog to stop pulling, and to sit and/or lie down. All dogs stop pulling and sit eventually. Most take only a couple of minutes; the all-time record is $22\frac{1}{2}$ minutes. Time how long it takes. Gently praise the dog when she stops pulling, and as soon as she

A well-trained Poodle will walk easily and calmly by your side.

sits, enthusiastically praise the dog and take just one step forwards, then immediately stand still. This single step usually demonstrates the ballistic reinforcing nature of pulling on leash; most dogs explode to the end of the leash, so be prepared for the strain. Stand firm and wait for the dog to sit again. Repeat this half a dozen times and you will probably notice a progressive reduction in the force of the dog's one-step explosions and a radical reduction in the time it takes for the dog to sit each time.

As the dog learns "Sit we go" and "Pull we stop," she will begin to walk forward calmly with each single step and automatically sit when you stop.

Now try two steps before you stop. Wooooooo! Scary! When the dog has mastered two steps at a time, try for three. After each success, progressively increase the number of steps in the sequence: Try four steps and then six, eight, ten and twenty steps before stopping. Congratulations! You are now walking the dog on leash.

Whenever walking with the dog (off leash or on leash), make sure you stop periodically to practice a few position commands and stays before instructing the dog to "Walk on!"

Integrating training into a walk offers 200 separate opportunities to use the continuance of the walk as a reward to reinforce the dog's education.

CHAPTER NINE

Resources

BOOKS

About Poodles

Dahl, Del. The Complete Poodle. New York: Howell Book House, 1994.

Donnelly, Kerry. Poodles. Neptune, NJ: TFH Publications, 1996.

Geeson, Eileen. The Complete Standard Poodle. New York: Howell Book House, 1998.

About Health Care

American Kennel Club. *American Kennel Club Dog Care and Training.* New York: Howell Book House, 1991.

Carlson, Delbert, DVM, and James Giffen, MD. *Dog Owner's Home Veterinary Handbook.* New York: Howell Book House, 1992.

DeBitetto, James, DVM, and Sarah Hodgson. *You & Your Puppy.* New York: Howell Book House, 1995.

Lane, Marion. *The Humane Society of the United States Complete Guide to Dog Care.* New York: Little, Brown & Co., 1998.

McGinnis, Terri. *The Well Dog Book.* New York: Random House, 1991.

Schwartz, Stephanie, DVM. *First Aid for Dogs: An Owner's Guide to a Happy Healthy Pet.* New York: Howell Book House, 1998.

Volhard, Wendy and Kerry L. Brown. *The Holistic Guide for a Healthy Dog.* New York: Howell Book House, 1995.

About Training

Ammen, Amy. *Training in No Time.* New York: Howell Book House,1995.

Benjamin, Carol Lea. *Mother Knows Best.* New York: Howell Book House, 1985.

Bohnenkamp, Gwen. *Manners for the Modern Dog.* San Francisco: Perfect Paws, 1990.

Dunbar, Ian, Ph.D., MRCVS. *Dr. Dunbar's Good Little Book.* James & Kenneth Publishers, 2140 Shattuck Ave. #2406, Berkeley, CA 94704. (510) 658-8588. Order from Publisher.

Evans, Job Michael. *People, Pooches and Problems.* New York: Howell Book House, 1991.

Palika, Liz. *All Dogs Need Some Training.* New York: Howell Book House, 1997.

Volhard, Jack and Melissa Bartlett. *What All Good Dogs Should Know: The Sensible Way to Train.* New York: Howell Book House, 1991.

About Activities

Hall, Lynn. *Dog Showing for Beginners.* New York: Howell Book House, 1994.

O'Neil, Jackie. *All About Agility.* New York: Howell Book House, 1998.

Simmons-Moake, Jane. *Agility Training, The Fun Sport for All Dogs.* New York: Howell Book House, 1991.

Vanacore, Connie. *Dog Showing: An Owner's Guide.* New York: Howell Book House, 1990.

Volhard, Jack and Wendy. *The Canine Good Citizen.* New York: Howell Book House, 1994.

MAGAZINES

THE AKC GAZETTE, The Official Journal for the Sport of Purebred Dogs American Kennel Club 260 Madison Ave. New York, NY 10016 www.akc.org

DOG FANCY Fancy Publications 3 Burroughs Irvine, CA 92618 (714) 855-8822 http://dogfancy.com

DOG WORLD Maclean Hunter Publishing Corp. 500 N. Dearborn, Ste. 1100 Chicago, IL 60610 (312) 396-0600 www.dogworldmag.com

PETLIFE: YOUR COMPANION ANIMAL MAGAZINE Magnolia Media Group 1400 Two Tandy Center Fort Worth, TX 76102 (800) 767-9377 www.petlifeweb.com

DOG & KENNEL 7-L Dundas Circle Greensboro, NC 27407 (336) 292-4047 www.dogandkennel.com

MORE INFORMATION ABOUT POODLES

National Breed Club

POODLE CLUB OF AMERICA
Corresponding Secretary:
Thomas W. Carneal
418 W. 2nd St.
Maryville, MO 64468
(660) 582-4955

Breeder Contact:
Richard Lehman
(956) 447-1939

Breed Rescue:
Helen Taylor
(409) 321-0132

The Club can send you information on all aspects of the breed, including the names and addresses of breed clubs in your area, as well as obedience clubs. Inquire about membership.

The American Kennel Club

The American Kennel Club (AKC), devoted to the advancement of pure-bred dogs, is the oldest and largest registry organization in this country. Every breed recognized by the AKC has a national (parent) club. National clubs are a great source of information on your breed. The affiliated clubs hold AKC events and use AKC rules to hold performance events, dog shows, educational programs, health clinics and training classes. The AKC staff is divided between offices in New York City and Raleigh, North Carolina. The AKC has an excellent Web site that provides information on the organization and all AKC-recognized breeds. The address is **www.akc.org**.

For registration and performance events information, or for customer service, contact:

THE AMERICAN KENNEL CLUB
5580 Centerview Dr., Suite 200
Raleigh, NC 27606
(919) 233-9767

The AKC's executive offices and the AKC Library (open to the public) are at this address:

THE AMERICAN KENNEL CLUB
260 Madison Ave.
New York, New York 10014
(212) 696-8200 (general information)
(212) 696-8246 (AKC Library)
www.akc.org

UNITED KENNEL CLUB
100 E. Kilgore Rd.
Kalamazoo, MI 49001-5598
(616) 343-9020
www.ukcdogs.com

AMERICAN RARE BREED ASSOCIATION
9921 Frank Tippett Rd.
Cheltenham, MD 20623
(301) 868-5718 (voice or fax)
www.arba.org

CANADIAN KENNEL CLUB
89 Skyway Ave., Ste. 100
Etobicoke, Ontario
Canada M9W 6R4
(416) 675-5511
www.ckc.ca

ORTHOPEDIC FOUNDATION FOR ANIMALS (OFA)
2300 E. Nifong Blvd.
Columbia, MO 65201-3856
(314) 442-0418
www.offa.org/

Trainers

Animal Behavior & Training Associates (ABTA)
9018 Balboa Blvd., Ste. 591
Northridge, CA 91325
(800) 795-3294
www.Good-dawg.com

Association of Pet Dog Trainers (APDT)
(800) PET-DOGS
www.apdt.com

National Association of Dog Obedience Instructors (NADOI)
729 Grapevine Highway, Ste. 369
Hurst, TX 76054-2085
www.kimberly.uidaho.edu/nadoi

89

Associations

Delta Society
P.O. Box 1080
Renton, WA 98507-1080
(Promotes the human/animal bond
through pet-assisted therapy and other
programs)
www.petsforum.com/
DELTASOCIETY/dsi400.htm

Dog Writers Association of America
(DWAA)
Sally Cooper, Secretary
222 Woodchuck Lane
Harwinton, CT 06791
www.dwaa.org

National Association for Search and
Rescue (NASAR)
4500 Southgate Place, Ste. 100
Chantilly, VA 20157
(703) 222-6277
www.nasar.org

Therapy Dogs International
6 Hilltop Rd.
Mendham, NJ 07945

OTHER USEFUL RESOURCES— WEB SITES

General Information— Links to Additional Sites, On-Line Shopping

www.k9web.com – resources for the dog
world

www.netpet.com – pet-related products,
software and services

www.apapets.com – The American Pet
Association

www.dogandcatbooks.com – book
catalogue

www.dogbooks.com – on-line bookshop

www.animal.discovery.com/ – cable
television channel on-line

Health

www.avma.org – American Veterinary
Medical Association (AVMA)

www.avma.org/care4pets/avmaloss.htm –
AVMA site dedicated to consideration of euthanizing sick pets and the
grieving process after losing a pet.

www.aplb.org – Association for Pet Loss
Bereavement (APLB)—contains an
index of national hot lines for on-line
and office counseling.

www.netfopets.com/AskTheExperts.
html – veterinary questions answered
on-line.

Breed Information

www.bestdogs.com/news/ – newsgroup

www.cheta.net/connect/canine/
breeds/ – Canine Connections Breed
Information Index